Ontario Provincial Parks

TRAIL GUIDE

Allen MacPherson

The BOSTON
MILLS PRESS

This book is dedicated to my grandchildren. May you learn to appreciate,
understand and protect our special places.

Copyright © 2000 by Allen MacPherson

Published in 2000 by
Boston Mills Press
132 Main Street
Erin, Ontario   N0B 1T0
Tel 519-833-2407
Fax 519-833-2195
e-mail books@bostonmillspress.com
www.bostonmillspress.com

An affiliate of
Stoddart Publishing Co. Limited
34 Lesmill Road
Toronto, Ontario, Canada
M3B 2T6
Tel 416-445-3333
Fax 416-445-5967
e-mail gdsinc@genpub.com

Distributed in Canada by
General Distribution Services Limited
325 Humber College Boulevard
Toronto, Canada M9W 7C3
Orders 1-800-387-0141 Ontario & Quebec
Orders 1-800-387-0172 NW Ontario
  & other provinces
e-mail cservice@genpub.com

Distributed in the United States by
General Distribution Services Inc.
PMB 128, 4500 Witmer Industrial Estates
Niagara Falls, New York 14305-1386
Toll-free 1-800-805-1083
Toll-free fax 1-800-481-6207
e-mail gdsinc@genpub.com
www.genpub.com

THE CANADA COUNCIL | LE CONSEIL DES ARTS
FOR THE ARTS | DU CANADA
SINCE 1957 | DEPUIS 1957

We acknowledge for their financial support of our publishing program the
Canada Council, the Ontario Arts Council, and the Government of Canada
through the Book Publishing Industry Development Program (BPIDP).

Canadian Cataloguing in Publication Data

MacPherson, Allen, 1949-
  Ontario provincial parks trail guide

Includes bibliographical references.
ISBN 1-55046-290-3

1. Nature trails - Ontario - Guidebooks.
2. Provincial parks and reserves - Ontario - Guidebooks.
I. Title.

QH58.M32 2000   508.713 C00-930498-3

Design by Walter J. Pick, Taylor Design Group
Printed in Canada

On the Spruce Boardwalk Trail in Algonquin Provincial Park.

Contents

Preface

Many people have written about our relationship with the wilderness, but two in particular mirror my way of thinking about nature. One is Ralph Waldo Emerson, who wrote, in *Nature*, that "The invariable mark of wisdom is to see the miraculous in the common." The other is Henry David Thoreau, who described his experiences when walking and wrote that "In wilderness is the preservation of the world." Nature can help us know ourselves, and at the same time is worth preserving for its own sake, as well as for the values we humans attach to it.

As we enter the 21st century, the 150-year-old words of these nature lovers are as relevant as ever. It is my belief this guidebook will allow you to contribute to both the appreciation and the protection of our natural world. It will also offer encouragement to park managers to increase their efforts to improve and maintain trail opportunities in our beautiful provincial parks.

This is the first comprehensive guide written for interpretive and hiking trails in Ontario provincial parks. Therefore, I ask you, the user, to write to me, care of the publisher whenever you discover a flaw in the trail descriptions or would like to share a special trail experience. I also encourage you to write to the relevant park superintendent as well to voice your opinions and concerns. After all, it is your park!

The photographs were taken by the author, or supplied by individuals or Ontario Parks. They were selected to illustrate the objective of the nature walk or an outstanding point of interest along the trail.

Allen MacPherson

Acknowledgments

I acknowledge the assistance of dozens of individuals who have provided me with the written and verbal information that allowed me to record the trail descriptions with a high degree of accuracy. The staff of the provincial parks, the natural heritage interpreters, park personnel and park (assistant) superintendents were important sources. Special thanks go to Ontario Parks project advisor Bob Moos. Others who provided special assistance include personal friends Cathy Sloat, Julia Schall, Dusan Nedelko, Gwen Brice, Angelo DiMondo, Nancy Checko, Bill Hagerty, Trish Manning, Lisa Harvey, "The Howarths," as well as acquaintances, supporters and contributors too numerous to mention individually. Sir Sandford Fleming College and Ontario Parks provided institutional support, and the Canadian Geographic Society provided a generous grant. And last, but not least, I thank my wife, Barbara, for understanding and sharing my love of our natural world.

Allen MacPherson
Lindsay, 2000

Introduction

This guide briefly describes the 302 interpretive and hiking trails found in 87 operating Ontario Provincial Parks. These trails range from those well-known and well-used in parks such as Algonquin, to little-known trails visited by only a few people. They lead you to explore rivers, waterfalls, caves, cliffs, rugged shorelines, forests, bogs and marshes, and traces of our history in abandoned farms, old mines, fire towers and native pictographs. You will become acquainted with the life and stories of a few of the early settlers, miners, loggers, trappers and the native peoples. You will also be able to add to the pleasure of walking by combining it with other pursuits — bird watching, the study of rocks, wildflowers, bogs, ferns, trees and other natural features. Best of all, you will come to know the land better, and increase your sense of connectedness to it and respect for all that it embraces.

The majority of the nature walks described are generally less than two hours long, easy to walk with clearly marked routes. Since the trails are located within a park, parking, toilets, and drinking water are either at the start of the trail or nearby. Descriptions of the trail are based upon information gathered during the summers of 1998–99 either from the park staff and/or during actual trail visits. However, you should be on the alert for possible changes due to human intervention and/or natural occurrences.

How to use this guide

This guide book can be used as a vacation planner, or as an education or adventure guide. Families or individuals can use this guidebook together with the *Ontario Parks Guide* to chose a park for a camping vacation, or a day visit. The educator can use this trail guidebook to plan school field trips matching self-guiding interpretive trail themes to school curriculum. The senior citizen can use the guide to determine where and what trails provide the best experience for their individual needs. Finally, the avid hiker can decide if she wants to get more information about an interesting hiking or backpacking trail for a particular park.

The provincial parks that do have trails are organized into six geographical tourist regions. The information listed for each park is the address, telephone and/or fax numbers, operating dates, location, natural features and trail attributes.

Four descriptors are used for quick and easy reference. The first divides the trails into three, general-use categories. The next identifies the trail difficulty, and the third and fourth give information on time and distance/direction.

The following terms are used to describe the trail categories:

 Interpretive trails are usually up to 120 minutes or approximately 1.0 to 4 km in length, and concentrate on one or more themes. Interpretive information is provided by means of either display panels or a printed guide booklet.

 Short hiking trails are usually 120 minutes or more and are 5 to 15 km in length. They do not necessarily concentrate on a theme or visitor education.

 Backcountry or backpacking trails are longer and hiking them will generally require one or more nights of camping. The word "map" is usually included, and this means that a detailed map is available from the park. You shouldn't hike a backcountry trail unless you have a compass and/or detailed park map or topographical map, along with the skills and ability to use them.

The following terms are used to rate the trail's level of difficulty:

Barrier-free
This is mostly in compliance with the Ontario Building Code, with no steep slopes, stairs, soft surfaces or other barriers. Suitable for wheelchairs, child strollers and other walking aids.

Easy
Suitable for those new to the activity of nature walking and hiking, those with minor physical impairments, or for young children accompanied by an adult. Can be walked with light footwear but high-topped boots are recommended. The trail is generally on easier surfaces (such as earth path, or wood chips) and less strenuous terrain. The trail route is easily followed.

Moderate
Suitable for fit persons with some previous experience. Proper footwear is recommended. Trail requires attention to the nature of the treadway surface, because roots, rocks and other obstacles may be present. Distance, speeds and exertion levels tend to be higher than for easy trails. The route is generally well marked.

Strenuous
The level of difficulty increases due to the nature of the surface and/or terrain and the distance to be covered. Suitable for fit, experienced and properly equipped hikers, as steep grades will be encountered. Detailed guidebooks and maps are recommended.

Very strenuous
This is similar to "strenuous" but requires frequent or almost continual care and/or exertion because of the surface, terrain, speed/distance and possibly weight of backpack. On certain terrain, you may need maps, compass and other route-finding skills.

Walking time and distance/direction are also given
Walking time is averaged time. It allows for only brief stops. Strong hikers may often beat the listed times, while the less active and experienced, or those who take extended breaks for nature study or photography, might find it takes longer to reach their destination.

The distances are either looped or linear. Linear distances include measurements both ways. Looped trails have been measured for total, round-trip distance. The measurements are based solely upon the information provided by Ontario Parks.

OTHER SPECIAL PLACES

Those regions with non-operating provincial parks that provide interpretive and hiking trails are listed at the end of some sections.

GLOSSARY OF TERMS

Throughout the guidebook certain terminology is used to describe some aspect of the natural environment or provincial parks operation. Its use provides accurate and concise information. I have kept the number of terms to as few as possible. Parks that have interpretive trail guides or panels provide easy-to-understand information about any of the natural or cultural features briefly identified in the text.

Boreal Forest
A type of northern hemisphere forest (also called coniferous), dominated by conifers and extending between the tundra to the north and a mixed forest of conifers and deciduous trees to the south.

Boreal Forest Region
In Ontario, this is the mainly coniferous forest that covers the northern portion of the Canadian Shield and Clay Belt to the treeline.

Canadian Shield
This refers to the ancient worn-down Precambrian rocks exposed at the surface. The Shield, sometimes called the Laurentian Shield, extends over two-fifths of the land area of Canada.

Carolinian Forest Region
This is the forest zone found in the most southerly parts of Ontario, immediately north of Lake Erie. It lies on the Great Lakes Lowland, is characterized by deciduous trees and is home to many species at or close to the northern distribution limits.

Coniferous
These are evergreen shrubs and trees, characterized by needle-shaped leaves, cones and a resinous wood.

Deciduous
This refers to trees or plants whose leaves fall when mature or at the end of the growing season.

Grades
Grades are slopes, climbs or ascents. The relative steepness and number of grades affects the trail rating. One short steep grade may not change the rating from "easy," but longer and more numerous grades will.

Great Lakes–St. Lawrence Forest Region
This refers to the band of mixed coniferous and deciduous trees found between the boreal forest to the north and the Carolinian Forest to the south. In Ontario

this forest type lies partly on the Canadian Shield and partly on the Great Lakes–St. Lawrence Lowland.

Operating season
This is the period when park services and facilities are operated. Fees are usually charged. Some non-operating parks offer trails and passive recreation, but will not normally offer toilets, meet park operating standards, or charge fees.

Stops
These are locations along the trail where there are either interpretative displays or numbered posts. If posts, printed trail guides containing corresponding numbered text is read at each post. Either method allows you to learn firsthand and at your own leisure the park's natural or cultural features.

Trail surface
This is the trail's walking surface, or tread. It can be level with few obstacles or have exposed roots and rocks to make travel more difficult. Trail ratings (from barrier-free to very strenuous) take this into account.

Many trails have boardwalks for easy access.

Take a hike

Hiking can be one of life's simple pleasures and one of the best ways to enjoy our natural surroundings. You don't need a lot of money, technical equipment or years of training; just a little planning, good common sense, a pair of comfortable, rugged shoes and concern for the environment are all that's needed for a great adventure.

The key to happy hiking is always to look after your feet. For easy trails, a good pair of walking shoes will suffice. In rugged or more remote areas on strenuous trails, a pair of hiking boots is recommended. A good outdoor equipment store can show you the wide range of styles and prices.

It is a good idea to carry a backpack, even for short easy trails. A lightweight day pack, preferably with padded straps, is ideal. In hot weather a belt pack or fanny pack is more comfortable because it allows your back to breathe and also avoids the problem of a stiff neck and sore shoulders. A couple could get all their necessary gear in one day pack and one fanny pack.

Plan ahead — select a trail that meets your level of experience. If you're unsure about your level, a trial run in your local area is a good idea. This will give you a chance to test or break-in equipment and give you experience reading a trail map. Once you've determined your skill level you're ready to select a trail. Guidebooks (like this one!), trail guides and maps can help you here, and most provincial parks have maps of their trails.

Whenever possible you should wait for a sunny day. The pleasures are much greater, and the problems more predictable. But even on sunny days the weather can change. Rain gear should always be carried in your hiking pack, no matter what the weather forecast. It only pours when you forget it! In hot weather, a wide-brimmed hat is better than a cap because it protects your neck and ears. A sunscreen is especially useful to help avoid sunburn. In cold weather, a hat and gloves are essential. Check with the Park Information Centres for the current weather forecast.

At home, store your hiking gear in your pack; that way you won't forget it when you go hiking. And use your ingenuity: take bug-catchers, field guides, a magnifying glass, or binoculars, to increase your fun on the trail.

Here are some essential items for your pack:

Sunblock: One that's recommended for adults and children.

Insect Repellent: There are now effective, all-natural repellents. Don't use repellents with higher than 30% DEET content on children. Loose clothing with a tight weave will protect most of your body from biting insects. Dark colours attract mosquitoes and blackflies, so avoid black, red, blue and dark-brown clothing. Wear light colours, but remember that both insects are very attracted to blue jeans!

Sunglasses: Good quality with sufficient UV protection.

Whistle: Sturdy and loud to attract attention in an emergency.

First Aid Kit: Commercial kits are available, or make your own.

Watch: To make sure everyone gets back on time.

Compass: To use with maps or trail guides, essential for backcountry trails.

Map/Trail Guide: Take a few minutes to go over your route with everyone before you start out. Call ahead to get the park to send you a map or guide.

Toilet Paper: For those emergencies. Walk off the trail, dig a small, shallow depression and cover up with leaves and soil.

Water and Snacks: Try not to let the kids deplete their own supplies, but save some for emergencies. In hot weather you will need a lot of water. Wide-mouthed screw-top litre-sized bottles are ideal. If you freeze them the night before you hike (leaving room at the top for expansion) and carry them wrapped in a towel you can have ice-cold water on the hottest day.

Camera: Finally, an inexpensive camera that kids can use will add immeasurably to their enjoyment of the great outdoors. It lets them create a visual record of their trip, and reinforces the outdoor enthusiast's credo, "Take only pictures, leave only footprints."

Hiking with kids

SOME DO'S AND DON'TS

Being prepared is the key to a successful hike with kids. Not just in terms of having the right equipment and information, but in your thinking and attitude as well. Remember, kids don't have as much endurance or strength as adults. They get cold more quickly, they're more active, more easily bored, and in their enthusiasm they often forget about safety issues. Keep in mind, when hiking with children, that the destination isn't as important as the process of getting there.

Make a realistic plan. Don't overestimate a child's abilities, don't overload children's backpacks if you're planning a short or backpacking hike, and choose an appropriate hike with easily achieved goals.

Set a slower pace. Allow time for frequent rests, give compliments and snacks along the way and encourage kids to stop and explore if something interests them.

Be flexible. Don't worry about adhering to a schedule. Be prepared to modify your plans en route. Listen to what the kids are saying and keep an open mind.

Encourage safety, responsibility and environmental awareness. Whenever possible explain rather than give orders (unless the safety of the child or the environment is at stake).

Be aware of dangers along the selected trails such as poison ivy or steep cliffs and take appropriate precautions.

Assess trail length and rating to assist you in deciding which trail to take for the age and ability of your child.

Don't forget about the child in a backpack carrier. In cool weather, baby will get cold more quickly since he or she is sitting still. Let baby out to crawl, walk or run on a regular basis.

TRAIL ACTIVITIES

Songs: This is a fun way to make the time on the trail slip away. Here are a few suggestions: "Going on a Lion Hunt," "I Love to Go A Wandering," "Heigh Ho, Heigh Ho," (from *Snow White and the Seven Dwarfs* — change the words to suit your destination), "The Ants Go Marching," "Land of the Silver Birch," etc.

Help your child select a hiking stick from the forest ground. Remember to use a fallen branch and return it to the forest.

Play rhymes and word games, like One, Two Buckle My Shoe, or create an I Spy list.

Scavenger hunt: If you're familiar with the trail and know the sort of nature items that will be seen, make up a list of things to be identified along the trail. For younger children this game works well if you give them a picture of the item (a maple leaf, on a recipe card, for example). Remember to encourage them to look and find, but not remove or destroy.

Nature rubbings: Take a few crayons and some paper and create some nature rubbings. Place the paper on a rock or tree surface and rub with the crayon. This is an easy nature craft for your child to take home and keep in a special place as a reminder of their hike.

Storytelling: Use stories about the people who lived and work in this area. Tell how they used trails as highways and sidewalks. Cloud gazing is a creative game to point out shapes and images in the clouds. This is usually best done during a rest stop and not while hiking!

Books: Bring along some of your child's favourite nature books. Refer to them on the trail. It will be easy to say at home, "Do you remember when we saw this on the trail?"

Bug trap: Bring along a purchased or homemade bug trap. This will allow the child to take a closer look at the live bugs you catch. When you're done, simply release the unharmed bugs where you found them.

Rules and regulations

You must purchase a permit to hike the nature trails in Ontario Provincial Parks. If you're visiting for the day this permit can be obtained upon entering the park or at a self fee station. Be sure the permit is displayed on your vehicle dashboard for the Wardens to see. If you're camping in the park, your campsite permit allows you use of the trails. It should be displayed on the car's dashboard.

It is recommended that all hikers stop by the park office before beginning any serious hiking. The office serves as a clearing house for all hiking activity in the park. In addition to issuing permits and registration forms, they dispense maps and up-to-date information on trail conditions and weather, and provide free publications covering everything from black bears to hypothermia. They also can inform hikers of any policy changes that may have occurred since the printing of this guide.

Other useful information

As well as the individual park addresses listed in the guide you can write to the following government office for further assistance:

Ministry of Natural Resources
Ontario Parks
Box 7000
300 Water Street
Peterborough, Ontario
K9J 8M5

Telephone numbers and websites
Current telephone numbers for all the parks are listed. If an internet web site address is known for a specific park it is provided. For more information about provincial parks call 1-800-667-1940 or visit their website at www.ontarioparks.com

Friends of Provincial Parks
These are community based, not-for-profit, charitable organizations that work to enhance the interpretive, educational and recreational objectives of the park with which they are associated. An association's activities include, but are not limited to, sponsoring of special events, developing and selling educational products such as trail guides and maps and appropriate souvenir items, fund-raising, and supporting research projects. For more information you can write to them. Addresses are listed at the back of the book.

Other trail organizations
Some of the provincial parks are linked to, or are part of, long-distance hiking trails such as the Bruce Trail. These long-distance hiking trails are operated and maintained by volunteer organizations, which often publish detailed guides, and welcome new members. A list of these organizations and addresses are provided at the back of the book.

Trail guides
These are either sold or provided free by individual parks. In parks where there is a Friends of Provincial Park organization they may produce and sell the interpretive

guides to raise funds for their activities in support of the park. The quality and information contained in these guides about the park's natural and cultural history is excellent. Write, call or visit their web site for a price list and mail-ordering form. Most of the trail guides are written in English, but some guides are available in French in designated areas. Parks that have guides in both languages are identified.

Ontario Parks Guide
This free guide is produced each spring by Ontario Parks. It is an excellent resource for planning your camping vacation. It is available in both English and French.

Maps
Parks that print a free park tabloid (information sheet) include a sketch map of all their trails. In addition, there are some excellent backpacking hiking trail maps sold by the park or the Friends of Provincial Park organizations. The trail descriptions identify those parks that do provide maps. Write, call or check the website to order them.

The avid backpacker who wants more detail can order topographical maps in a choice of scales from the Ministry of Natural Resources Information Office in Toronto or Peterborough. Call 1-800-667-1940, or purchase them locally at park information centres and official map dealers in certain urban areas.

Further reading
A suggested reading list is provided at the back of the book. Most of these books were consulted in writing this guide.

Adopt-a-trail programs
Adopt-a-trail programs run in some parks allow groups and individuals to assist in maintaining and cleaning-up trails frequently used by the general public. This is done in co-operation with the Provincial Park and Friends of Provincial Park organizations. If you are interested in volunteering, contact the park or a Friends organization and ask if they have an adopt-a-trail program for their park.

Hiking season

Most parks and their trails are open from May until September, but many have longer operating seasons. The *Parks Guide* published by Ontario Parks provides operating dates for each park. Conducted nature walks are provided during July and August. Other trail opportunities such as mountain biking or cross-country skiing are mentioned under name of the specific park. Contact the park directly for information about these trails. When parks are not operating, their entrance is usually gated. However, in many cases you can park at the gate and enjoy a walk in the park. Trails may not be maintained, so during the off-season trees may block the trail, signs may not be posted, staff are not monitoring trail use, and so on. Hikers should take extra care if they use a trail when the park is not officially open.

Tips for safe hiking

Bears may feel threatened if surprised. Hike in a group and make loud noises, whistle, talk, sing or carry a noise-maker such as bells or a can containing stones. Most bears will leave if they are aware of your group's presence. Stay in the open as much as possible. Keep children close at hand on trails. Be especially alert when travelling into the wind — the bear may not get your scent and be warned of your presence. In dense bush and near rushing water, don't depend on your noisemaker being heard. Finally, it is always good practice to check at park information centres to get a current report on bear activity.

Giardia lamblia "Beaver fever or purple burps" is a waterborne parasite that can cause severe diarrhea infection. Giardia is carried by many animals but the human infective strain is most frequently found in beavers, domestic dogs and, of course, humans. The parasite finds its way into water, rivers, streams or ponds. Beavers and muskrats are common sources of giardia parasite, because they live and defecate in the water. When hiking, take your own water or boil your drinking water for at least five minutes.

Wood ticks are small, flat-bodied insects that require a meal of mammal blood as part of their reproductive cycle. Some species may transmit Lyme Disease, a serious illness first characterized by an inflamed, red ring around a tick bite. The best precaution is to wear long pants, keep moving and examine yourself frequently.

Black flies are active and irritating from mid-May to late June, during warm days, particularly active during evening. They do stop biting when the sun sets.

Mosquitoes are active from May to mid-August, especially during the last few hours of the day.

Deer flies commonly attack your head, and their bite can cause a large, reactive swelling.

Poison ivy is commonly found in the parks. If there is one plant whose appearance you should get to know, this is it. The irritant on its leaves causes an itchy and painful rash, and people vary in their sensitivity to it. Remember the rule: "Leaflet three, let it be."

Scenic view along the trail at Lake Superior Provincial Park.

Some final words

Plan ahead. Choose trips you are in shape to handle. Allow time for unexpected events and changes to your route and itinerary.

Stay on the trail even if it occasionally means muddy boots. Going around obstacles creates parallel trails and widens existing trails. Utilize switchbacks to minimize erosion and conserve your energy. Shortcuts quickly become erosion gullies.

Pack out all garbage. Whenever possible pack out litter that previous less considerate visitors have left behind.

Always leave rocks, flowers and all other natural objects where you find them.

Minimize disturbance of stones, soil and plant life. Never pick wildflowers or edible plants.

Where facilities are not provided, one's toilet should be well away from trails, lakes and streams. Dig a small pit (no more than 15 cm deep) bury toilet paper and restore the ground as closely as possible to its original state. Improper disposal of human waste is a major factor contributing to the spread of giardia in North America.

Never feed or harass wildlife. It is illegal and harmful to the animal's health, and alters their natural behaviour. Observe all wildlife from a distance: do not disturb or entice.

While they are permitted on a leash, dogs are a threat to wildlife, and are an aesthetic intrusion for other visitors. They are often carriers of giardia if allowed to wander. Please keep your dog at home, under close control or at the campsite.

A last word: The Ministry of Natural Resources (Ontario Parks) is responsible for the establishment, maintenance and marking of all trails. There are some trails in need of maintenance and signs. It is hoped that this guide will generate interest in, and support for, the continuing improvements of provincial park trails.

NORTHWESTERN REGION

PARKS OF THE REGION

Aaron
Blue Lake
Caliper Lake
Kakabeka Falls
Lake of the Woods
MacLeod

Neys
Ojibway
Ouimet Canyon
Pakwash
Pigeon River
Quetico

Rainbow Falls
Rushing River
Sandbar Lake
Sleeping Giant

AARON PROVINCIAL PARK

Box 730, Dryden, Ontario P8N 2Z4

Information: Call 807 938-6534 (summer)
807 223-5702 (winter)
Fax 807 223-2092

Operating season: May to September

Location: This park is located east of the new Dryden city limits on Highway 17.

Natural features: The park's Thunder Lake is a remnant of ancient glaciers that covered Ontario tens of thousands of years ago. Fringing the lake are mixed forests of aspen, jack pine, white cedar and balsam, typical of the boreal region. The forest is home to moose, white-tailed deer and black bear.

Both trails are looped, 0.5 m wide, and travel over an earth path.

Eastern White Cedar Trail

Interpretive guide   Easy   1 hour   1.2 km

 The Cedar Trail travels through a mixed stand of mature and young trees, and a descriptive guide highlights some of the trees and plants typical of the area.

The Aspen Trail

Interpretive guide   Easy   1 hour   1.9 km

An interpretive guide with eight stops explains the trees and birdlife of a boreal forest.

BLUE LAKE PROVINCIAL PARK

Box 730, Dryden, Ontario P8N 2Z4

Information: Call 807 227-2601
807 223-3341
Fax 807 223-2824

Operating season: May to September

Location: The park is approximately 48 km northwest of Dryden and is accessible from Highway 17.

Natural features: Blue Lake, which is 27 m deep in places, is so clear that you can see the bottom at a depth of six metres. Lady's slipper and starflowers bloom in the forests, which are also home to a variety of small animals and birds.

All three trails are looped and a minimum of 0.5 m wide. Two trails have earth paths. Conducted nature walks are offered.

Spruce Fen Trail *

Interpretive guide   Barrier-free   45 minutes   1 km

Travelling over a boardwalk, you come to a spruce fen. There are seven interpretive stops on this trail, explaining the ecology of the area.

*Al's Picks, see page 43.

Boulder Ridge Trail

Interpretive displays   Easy   45 minutes   1 km

As you walk this trail you will see how glaciers affected the landscape, and how forest fires have affected plant succession.

Rock Point Trail

Hiking   Moderate   2 hours   4 km

Along this trail you will be able to see glacial features such as a humpback, erratics, and pegmatites. As it takes you between Blue and Langton Lakes, the trail will wind through a variety of vegetation, highlighted by mature white cedar trees.

CALIPER LAKE PROVINCIAL PARK
Box 188, Nestor Falls, Ontario P0X 1K0

Information: Call 807 484-2181
              Fax 807 484-2227

Operating season: May to September

Location: The park is north of Lake of the Woods, accessible via Highways 17 and 71 from Thunder Bay.

Natural features: Rocky outcrops, and mature forests of white and red pine border the lake. American white pelicans, bald eagles and other species of bird can be seen from May to September.

Beaver Pond Trail

Interpretive guide   Moderate   1.5 or 3 hours   2.7 or 4 km

This 1.0-m-wide earth path trail has a double loop and interpretive stops to explore the park's boreal forest, beaver pond and rocky outcrops.

KAKABEKA FALLS PROVINCIAL PARK
Box 252, Kakabeka Falls, Ontario P0T1W0

Information: Call 807 473-9231
                  Fax 807 473-5973

Operating season: Open all year (day use)
                  May to October (camping)

Location: The park is located along Highway 11/17, 32 km west of Thunder Bay.

Natural features: The park is dominated by a single, spectacular feature — Kakabeka Falls — which drops 39 m over sheer cliffs. Some of the world's oldest fossils, formed 1.6 billion years ago, can be found in the gorge below the falls.

There are seven trails — three looped and four linear. All the trails are a minimum of 0.5 m wide, travelling over a variety of surfaces from earth path, to gravel or boardwalk. Conducted nature walks are offered. Other trail uses are mountain biking, auto trail and cross-country skiing.

Poplar Point Trail

Hiking/Map   Easy   2 hours   3.6 km

This trail is 3 m wide and shared with automobiles. It loops through a dense poplar and white birch forest.

Contact Trail

| Hiking | Easy | 30 minutes | 1 km |

The route of this trail is sometimes ill-defined, often travelling over bare rock. Along the trail you will encounter a series of small waterfalls. As well, you will see remnants of glacial processes and of the logging operations that were once carried out on the Kaministiquia River.

Little Falls Trail

| Hiking | Strenuous | 2 hours | 3 km |

Travelling along the rim of the west gorge of the Kaministiquia River valley, the route features a scenic lookout, a steep descent into the river valley, the picturesque Little Falls, and a final 30-m ascent to the historic Mountain Portage.

Mountain Portage Walking Trail*

| Interpretive displays | Barrier-free | 45 minutes | 1.25 km |

Travelling over a compacted gravel surface, you will visit seven interpretive display panels, plenty of resting benches, two map panels and three viewing points. The panels discuss the use of the area by native peoples, explorers and voyageurs, as well as the Canadian Armed Forces. Spectacular views of the river and gorge can be enjoyed from the trail.

*Al's Picks, see page 44.

River Terrace Loop Trail

| Hiking/Map | Moderate | 2 hours | 3.6 km |

From this trail, there are excellent views of the Kam River, and examples of two striking landforms — mesas and buttes. Varying soils encourage growth of a diversity of tree species, including the burr oak.

Beaver Meadows Trail

| Hiking/Map | Moderate | 2.5 hours | 11 km (return) |

Trail users travel to a beaver meadow, then wind down to the Kaministiquia River. The route follows the riverbank, so that walkers are close to the river and its surroundings.

Kakabeka Falls Trail

Interpretive displays   Easy   45 minutes   1 km (one way)

This boardwalk trail is located on both sides of the Kaministiquia River. There are four viewing areas on the east side, with seven interpretive panels, while the west side has two viewing areas and two display panels. The panels describe the history and folklore of the Falls. Sometimes known as the Little Niagara Falls, the Kakabeka Falls are 39 m high and 71 m wide.

LAKE OF THE WOODS PROVINCIAL PARK
R.R. 1, Sleeman, Ontario P0W 1M0

Information: Call 807 488-5531
             Fax   807 468-2737

Operating season: May to September

Location: This park is 43 km north of Rainy River near the borders of Ontario, Manitoba and Minnesota. Take Highway 621 north from Highway 11.

Natural features: The park lies within a transition zone of three discrete natural environments — northern, southern and prairie. The forest includes southern hardwoods such as elm and ash, as well as species with northern affinities such as spruce and jack pine. The mix of species is also evident in the park's birdlife. Species near the limit of their breeding ranges include pelicans, the yellow-headed blackbird and the western meadowlark.

Indian Head Point Trail

Interpretive displays   Easy   1 hour   1.6 km

This looped trail is 1.0 m wide and travels over an earth path. There are a number of interpretive displays describing some of the flora and fauna of the area. Eventually the trail arrives at a viewing tower overlooking Oscar's Bay on Lake of the Woods. Visitors can often see white pelicans from this spot.

MACLEOD PROVINCIAL PARK

Box 640, Geraldton, Ontario P0T 1M0

Information: Call 807 854-0370
                     Fax 807 887-2993

Operating dates: May to September

Location: The park is about 8 km east of Geraldton and about 25 km west of Longlac on Highway 1.

Natural features: The park's trees are mainly trembling aspen. Animals such as fox and moose are found here, and birds include red-eyed vireos, ovenbirds and northern warblers.

Park Trail

Hiking   Easy   30 minutes   1 km

This linear trail is 1.0 m wide, with an earth surface. It passes through a forest of trembling aspen, the predominant tree in the park.

NEYS PROVINCIAL PARK

Box 280, Terrace Bay, Ontario P0T 2W0

Information: Call 807 229-1624
                     Fax 807 229-1080

Operating Season: May to September

Location: The park is on a peninsula extending into Lake Superior, 26 km west of Marathon, off Highway 17.

Natural features: The park juts into Lake Superior from its scenic north shore. The rocky landscape has been shaped into interesting rock forms with potholes being carved out of the bedrock by the turbulent lake waters. The park is home to a small herd of rare woodland caribou, among the last of their kind in the region. Other wildlife includes moose, bears, wolves, deer and fox. The forest is dominated by spruce, red pine, balsam fir, white birch and trembling aspen. Lake Superior's cold waters provide a suitable microclimate for sub-arctic plants such as crowberry, bilberry and encrusted saxifrage.

The park was immortalized by the famous Group of Seven painters. The remoteness of the peninsula prompted the Canadian government to build a German prisoner-of-war camp here during World War II.

All the trails have a minimum 0.5-m width, and surfaces are mixed, from sandy beach to rock and earth path. Conducted nature walks are offered. All trails have interpretive display panels.

Dune Trail

Interpretive displays   Easy   45 minutes   1.5 km

This looped trail travels through a sand dune and boreal forest area. There are 12 interpretive panels explaining the succession of plants and trees that grow in these two distinct environments.

Lookout Trail

Interpretive displays   Moderate   1.5 hours   2.5 km

This trail takes you through a variety of habitats including sand dunes, rocky outcrops and forests. There is a viewing point with a spectacular view of Lake Superior. Along the way, there are ten panels explaining the plants and animals of the boreal forest, before the trail loops back to the start.

A conducted nature walk.

Point Trail

Interpretive displays   Easy   1 hour   2 km (return)

This trail twists and turns until it reaches a sandy shoreline. At the beach you walk along the shore, then re-enter the forest to find Prisoner's Point. At the Point, there are two interpretive display panels that give a brief history of the area.

Under the Volcano Trail *

Interpretive displays   Moderate   1.5 hours   1 km (return)

This linear trail travels over both rugged and smooth rock along the shore of Lake Superior. There are 11 interpretive display panels with information on the unique geology and geomorphology of the park. The panels are very informative and the scenery is dramatic, so the hike is well worth the effort. Care should be taken when scrambling over these and other wet rocks, as they may be slippery. Appropriate footwear is essential.

*Al's Picks, see page 47.

OJIBWAY PROVINCIAL PARK
Box 730, Dryden, Ontario P8N 2Z4

Information: Call 807 737-2033 (summer)
                807 934-2233 (winter)
         Fax 807 223-2824

Operating season: May to September

Location: About 25 km southwest of Sioux Lookout, near Highway 72 in northwest Ontario.

Natural features: Labrador tea, wild rice, lady's slipper, water lily, moss, lichen — these plants flourish in various sections of the boreal forest. There are moose, black bear and otter in the interior of the park, and campers report hearing the howling of wolves.

Four of the six trails are looped. All the trails are a minimum of 0.5 m wide, travelling over rock and earth paths with one boardwalk section.

Boreal Walking Trail

Hiking   Easy   1 hour   1.5 km

This short, looped hiking trail allows you to experience the essence of a boreal forest, with species such as larch and jack pine growing among white and black spruce and white birch. The trail leads across a footbridge to an island, and ends at a viewing area overlooking Little Vermilion Lake.

Red Pine Walking Trail

Interpretive guide   Easy   45 minutes   0.5 km

This trail climbs a hill and descends to a park road. It has nine interpretive stops explaining forest succession, and mapping the changes in forest type and size, including the succession from red to white pine.

Lakeshore Trail

Interpretive guide   Moderate   2.5 hours   6 km (return)

This linear trail has four interpretive stops explaining the different types of vegetation and geology found along the shore of the lake.

Ridge Bottom Trail

Interpretive guide   Moderate   1.5 hours   2.8 km

Some of the oldest rock in the world lies beneath your feet. A variety of lichens, soils and fungi are described along the trail at 14 interpretive stops.

Little Walking Trail

Interpretive guide   Easy   45 minutes   0.8 km

Twelve interpretive stops focus on the diversity of tree and plant species as well as the animal life typical of a boreal forest.

Terry Lake Trail

Hiking   Easy   1 hour   1.5 km (return)

This linear trail provides access to Terry Lake for fishing or for watching wildlife.

OUIMET CANYON PROVINCIAL PARK

Box 5000, Thunder Bay, Ontario P7C 5G6

Information: Call 807 977-2526
          Fax 807 977 2583

Operation season: May to September

Location: 60 km northeast of Thunder Bay on Highway 11/17, to Ouimet Canyon Road.

Natural features: This dramatically steep-sided canyon is one of Ontario's scenic wonders. It supports an unusual group of rare arctic-alpine plants on the deeply shaded valley floor. Here a microclimate similar to that a thousand miles to the north prevails. Fir-club moss and lichen, arctic pyrola and encrusted saxifrage are just some of the plant species flourishing here.

There is just one trail, and two trail map signs provide you with directions. After Canadian Thanksgiving in early October, visitors can reach the trailhead by parking 3 km away and walking the steep paved roadway to the trail.

Ouimet Canyon Trail

Interpretive displays   Easy   45 minutes   1 km

This looped, 2-m-wide trail travels over a compacted gravel surface. There are a few steep grades, and rest benches are provided. At the two viewing platforms extending over the edge of the canyon wall, detailed display panels explain how the canyon was formed and give information on the unique plant life. The view is unforgettable.

PAKWASH PROVINCIAL PARK

Box 928, Ear Falls, Ontario P0V 1T0

Information: Call 807 222-2059
             807 222-3346 (Park)
          Fax 807 222-3147

Operating season: May to September

Location: The park is 200 km north of Dryden on Highway 105.

Natural features: The park's marshes, bogs, sandy ridges and high cliffs of silt and clay are visible reminders of a former glacial lake. The area features a mixed forest of spruce, jack pine, birch and poplar, and supports a variety of wildlife including moose, black bear, deer and otter.

Nature Trail

Interpretive guide   Moderate   2 hours   5.1 km

This looped, 1.5-m-wide trail, of earth path and boardwalk, passes through a boreal forest full of blueberries, strawberries and cranberries. There are nine interpretive stops with information on the local flora and fauna.

PIGEON RIVER PROVINCIAL PARK
435 James Street South, Suite 221, Thunder Bay, Ontario P7E 6S8

Information: Call 807 964-2097
                   807 475-1531
          Fax   807 473-5973

Operating season: June to September

Location: Near the Minnesota border just west of Lake Superior, 50km south of Thunder Bay on Highway 61. The campground is 2 km west of Highway 61 along Highway 593.

Natural features: The park is characterized by a spectacular river gorge and the two dramatic cataracts of High Falls and Middle Falls. Burr oak, red maple, black ash and white elm are southern species of tree that mingle with the predominant species of a boreal forest.

Both trails are linear, 0.5 m wide, with an earth surface.

Lookout Trail

Hiking/Map   Strenuous   1.5 hours   2.7 km (return)

The trail ascends, sometimes steeply, to the top of a cliff overlooking Lake Superior,

Pigeon River and the surrounding area. Animal tracks and a variety of plant life can be spotted by the observant hiker.

High Falls Trail

Hiking/Map	Moderate	1.5 hours	2.6 km (return)

This trail takes you to the border between Canada and the United States, and one of northwestern Ontario's most beautiful sights — the highest falls in Minnesota. The trail starts on the north side of the Tourist Information building on Highway 61, travels along the highway, then dives underneath it to become the main trail. Walking down to the river, you turn right at an old stone chimney and follow the Pigeon River to the lower falls. Climbing to the top of the falls you will see the gorge and an old sluiceway. The first section of trail is level, then the climb to the top of the falls has irregular, steep grades.

Old Logging Road Trail

Hiking	Strenuous	2 hours	2.2 km

This trail connects with the High Falls and Lookout trails. A remnant of an old logging road, it is one of many that were once used to transport the timber, which was then floated down the Pigeon River. The section of trail near the scenic lookout is steep. It is also particularly noted for sightings of moose, deer and beaver.

QUETICO PROVINCIAL PARK
Atokokan, Ontario P0T 1C0

Information: Call 807 597-2735
             Fax   807 597-6185

Operating season: May to October

Location: This park is located about 160 km west of Thunder Bay off Highway 11, and extends south to the Minnesota border.

Natural features: Although some of the most interesting natural features are accessible only by canoe, there are trails near the park's main entrance. The park is noted for its limitless forests, mirror-smooth lakes and innumerable bogs, all supporting a rich variety of plants and animals. It is a boreal forest with pockets of southern trees such as oak, elm and silver maple, as well as magnificent stands of red and white pine. Large mammals, such as moose, bear and wolves live here, and in the summer more than 90 species of birds nest in the park.

Two of the seven trails are looped. All trails are a minimum of 0.5 m wide, over earth path. Conducted nature walks are offered, and there are cross-country skiing and snowshoeing trails.

Beaver Meadows Nature Trail

Hiking   Moderate   1 hour   2.5 km

This looped trail provides an opportunity for you to explore a variety of plant communities, and to see the effects of thin topsoil, insect infestations and forest fires.

Whiskeyjack Nature Trail

Hiking   Moderate   1 hour   2.5 km

This trail is known as the gateway to Quetico's wilderness. It begins on a boardwalk stretching through a forest-covered lowland of black spruce, Labrador tea and horsetail, then becomes an earth path meandering through diverse habitats.

Pickerel Point Trail

Hiking   Moderate   30 minutes   1.6 km (return)

This linear trail follows the Pickerel River upstream. You will have an opportunity to explore the aquatic and terrestrial plant life along the river banks, and to see bald eagles, kingfishers and ospreys.

French Falls Trail

Hiking   Strenuous   1 hour   2.4 km (return)

The trail offers several viewing points along its route, providing clear views of the Falls. On a historical note, in 1870 this was a resting area for over 1,400 troops who were en route to try to quell the Metis rebellion in Manitoba.

Pines Hiking Trail

Backpacking/   Strenuous   3.5 hours   10 km (return)
Hiking or overnight

Along this trail you can enjoy majestic old-growth red and white pines, picnic along the sandy beaches of Pickerel Lake, or venture further into the interior to camp.

Pickerel River Trail

Hiking	Barrier-free	30 minutes	1.6 km (return)

The trail meanders over a boardwalk through open areas, and into the forest. As you follow the lowlands of the Pickerel River, you will see alder, spruce and balsam fir. The trail then slowly ascends to the highlands of pine and birch. By the side of the trail are lookouts with quotations on the wilderness by writers, poets, conservationists and philosophers.

French Portage Trail

Hiking	Easy	2 hours	5 km (return)

The significance of this trail lies in its cultural history. First established by the native peoples and later used by European explorers and fur traders, it was a major highway to Manitoba and the west.

RAINBOW FALLS PROVINCIAL PARK

Box 280, Whitesand Lake, Terrace Bay, Ontario P0T 2W0

Information: Call 807 824-2298
Fax 807 824-3379

Operating season: May to September

Location: Between Schreiber and Rossport off Highway 17, on the north shore of Lake Superior.

Natural features: The falls themselves are the central feature, tumbling over multi-ledged granite bedrock. The river zigzags over a series of ledges, so that the water falls in cascades, rather than in one steep drop. When the sun is shining, a rainbow glows through the mist. The surrounding forest is boreal, with plants such as scarlet bunchberry and yellow clintonea.

All three trails are linear, up to a metre wide, and with an earth path or boardwalk surface. There is also a link to a 50-km section of the Voyageur Long Distance Hiking Trail, the Casque-Isles section. Cross-country ski trails are available during certain months.

Rainbow Falls Trail

Interpretive displays	Strenuous	30 minutes	1 km
		or 1.5 hours	3 km

For half a kilometre the trail runs over boardwalk and stairways along the Whitesand River, providing views of a series of cascading waterfalls. After descending nearly 60 m by a stairway, the trail bridges the river itself. There are three interpretive signs along the route, with information on the geology of the river and its surroundings.

Visitors have a choice at the bridge: they can either hike the remaining section over a rugged earth path, with very steep grades, or take an 8.8-km connecting trail to the Voyageur Long Distance Hiking Trail. The first choice will take them past ten interpretive display panels on the flora of the region, the trail ending at two lookout points with panoramic views of the park and Lake Superior. The second option is to take the Long Distance wilderness trail, maintained by a not-for-profit organization. To date this group has opened 600 km of trail, which, when complete, will be 1,100 km long. This connecting link is linear, so hikers must leave time to backtrack to their starting point.

Voyageur Hiking Trail (Casque-Isles section)

Backpacking	Strenuous	20 hours	52 km (return)

Hikers access this trail from within the park by the Rainbow Falls Trail, or can continue their trip west to Rossport or east to Terrace Bay. This west section follows the northern shoreline of Lake Superior.

The Back Forty Trail

Hiking	Strenuous	2.5 hours	5.6 km (return)

Hikers travel through black spruce, poplar and white birch to reach a viewing point overlooking Whitesand Lake. There are many steep climbs.

The Superior Trail

Hiking	Moderate	1 or 2 hours	4.8 km (return)

The trail winds along the top of a granite rock ridge to a lookout providing spectacular views of Lake Superior.

RUSHING RIVER PROVINCIAL PARK

Box 5080, Kenora, Ontario P9N 3X9

Information: Call 807 548-4351 (Park)
                      807 468-2669 (off season)
                Fax 807 468-2737
Operating Season: May to September

Location: The park is on Highway 71, approximately 20 km southeast of Kenora.

Natural features: The forest is dominated by jack pines of a uniform height. The heat from a forest fire in 1910 cracked open the pine cones, and the heat-resistant seeds all germinated at the same time, producing this unusual effect. Balsam, spruce, aspen and alder grew up among the pines, and produced a dense forest canopy shading a community of plant life that includes many edibles, such as blueberries, cherries, hazelnuts, raspberries and strawberries. Black bear, moose, and deer are seen occasionally, and the bird community includes more than 60 species, among them the great blue herons, loons and belted kingfishers.

Both trails are looped, one metre wide, and mostly earth path. Conducted nature walks are offered.

Beaver Pond Trail

| Hiking | Easy | 45 minutes | 1.5 km |

The trail circles an active beaver pond filled with water lily pads.

Lower Rapids Trail

| Hiking | Easy | 45 minutes | 2.0 km |

This trail takes you past rushing rapids and a number of small scenic waterfalls.

SANDBAR LAKE PROVINCIAL PARK

Box 730, Dryden, Ontario P8N 2Z4

Information: Call 807 934-2995 (Park)
807 223-7535
Fax 807 934-2325

Operating season: May to September

Location: The park is just off Highway 17, about 12 km northeast of Ignace, along Highway 599.

Natural features: Sandbar Lake is the largest of the ten lakes within the park's boundary. It has a long and narrow sandy beach. The remains of log dwellings and other artifacts from the late 1800s are evidence of the more recent past. The forest marks the transition zone between the Great Lakes–St. Lawrence and Boreal areas. Bluebeard lily, red bunchberry and various orchids grow on the forest floor, and the park has become known for its spotted sandpipers, darting across the beach in unmistakable, rapid runs.

Sandbar Silhouette Trail

Interpretive guide   Moderate   1 hour   1.6 km

The trail is an earth path, 1.5 m wide, which runs through a boreal forest area with mature red pine trees. There are 12 silhouettes explaining the local vegetation, and a section of the trail takes you to a clear view of the beach and lake.

SLEEPING GIANT PROVINCIAL PARK

General Delivery, Pass Lake, Ontario P0T 2M0

Information: Call 807 977-2526
807 475-1506
Fax 807 977-2583

Operating season: May to October
January to March

Location: The park is located on a peninsula jutting into Lake Superior, east of Thunder Bay. Take secondary road 587 south from Highway 11/17.

Natural features: The park is situated on rugged Sibley Peninsula. It features thick forests, many lakes, high rock cliffs and the most dramatic heights and lookouts in the province. Deep valleys and clear, fast-running streams characterize the terrain. The geology of the park is based on a series of layered sedimentary rock, with once-molten igneous rock squeezed between the layers. The park's name is derived from the Sleeping Giant, a series of mesas with a unique profile that gave rise to the well-known Ojibwa legend.

Due to the park's location, at a transition point between climatic zones, a great variety of plants, some rare, grow here. Arctic species such as cloudberry and bistort are found in the park, as are two rare orchids, the adder's mouth and striped, round-leaved orchis. Altogether, some 24 species of orchid grow here, and ferns of many types abound. The park's mammals include white-tailed deer, red fox, porcupine, moose, beaver, wolf and lynx. There have been 190 species of bird recorded, especially warblers.

There are seven interpretive trails and 11 short, backpacking trails in the park. Most of the hiking trails are backpacking, and follow the cliffs and coast.

The climax of a trip into the park's interior is, without a doubt, a climb up onto the Sleeping Giant. Standing on top of the highest vertical cliffs in Ontario (250 m), you will not only have breathtaking panoramic views, but will also gain a perspective of the area's essential character.

Unless otherwise stated, all the trails are 0.5 m to 1.5 m wide, with earth and rock surfaces. There is a trail map available at the Marie Louise Campground. Visitors should stop at the park's visitor centre to pick up information on the park's natural and cultural history before starting to walk the trails. Other types of trails available include cycling trails, a 12-km auto drive trail and over 60 km of cross-country ski trails. Conducted nature walks are offered.

Joe Creek Nature Trail

Interpretive displays   Moderate   1.5 hours   2.4 km

This looped trail has 19 interpretive stops along its length, describing a variety of natural features. It leads from Highway 587 to a series of small waterfalls, and is known for its variety of woodland flowers. After crossing a small footbridge, the trail returns to the highway on the other side of the creek.

Piney Wood Hills Nature Trail

Interpretive displays   Moderate   1 hour   4.8 km (return)

This linear trail winds through open mixed forest, then into forested, hilly terrain, ending at a good viewing point overlooking Joeboy Lake. The stands of red and white pine are the oldest in the park. The ten interpretive stops deal mostly with information on pine trees and the habits and habitat of moose.

Plantain Lane Trail

Hiking   Barrier-free   45 minutes   1.3 km (return)

Following the abandoned Silver Islet Road, this trail takes you over a small bridge on Sibley Creek. Although this trail is promoted as barrier-free, some trail users may need some assistance.

Ravine Lake Trail

Hiking   Moderate   1.5 hours   2.4 km

This combination loop and linear trail climbs steadily to two lookouts overlooking Grassy Lake and the peninsula's south coast. It then travels down to the shore of peaceful Ravine Lake, returning to the trailhead through a shaded cedar grove. The descent to the lake is steep and hikers should take care.

Sibley Creek Nature Trail

Interpretive displays   Easy   1.5 hours   1.7 km

This combination linear and loop trail leads you through a mixed forest to a marsh and stream. There are 20 interpretive displays that explain some aspect of the natural features along the trail, such as tree variety, beaver habitat and waterfowl.

Thunder Bay Bogs Nature Trail

Interpretive displays   Easy   45 minutes   0.8 km

This combination loop and linear trail crosses a rocky environment to the shores of a small, placid lake. Eighteen interpretive stops highlight glacial features and explain how plants adapt to these harsh growing conditions.

Wildlife Habitat Nature Trail

Hiking   Easy   2 hours   2.4 km

This looped trail weaves through an area altered for the purpose of creating a habitat for moose, and providing firewood for campers. A wildlife enclosure on the trail also allows visitors to see the impact that animals have on their habitat. This is part of an ongoing experiment to help determine some of the eating habits of certain species of animals.

These trail descriptions cover some of the interior short- and long-distance hiking trails. The distance and times indicated are one way. Most are not looped trails so careful planning is necessary. Be sure to refer to park trail maps for route layout.

The Kabeyun Trail

Hiking   Strenuous   4–6 hours   40 km
Backpacking   Very strenuous   or 3 days

This linear trail can be accessed from a number of other trails within the park, allowing you a choice of a day hike, or overnight camp. The scenery along the route is spectacular, and with Lake Superior always within reach, there are plenty of beaches and coves to relax in. Great care should be taken at the end of the peninsula, especially in wet weather, where the trail travels over boulders.

The Burma Trail

Hiking   Strenuous   4–6 hours   9.6 km

This linear trail passes through stands of mature red and white pine, by the shores of a number of small interior lakes, and over a variety of rocky outcrops. It is especially rewarding for birdwatchers.

Gardner Lake Trail

Hiking   Moderate   1 hour   2.4 km

This linear earth path is known for its moose-viewing opportunities. The trail takes you to Gardner Lake down to the remains of an old logging road. There are damp sections of this trail, so wear appropriate boots.

Sawbill Lake Trail

Hiking   Moderate   1 hour   2.4 km

This linear trail follows an old logging road and joins up with Sawyer Bay Trail.

Sawyer Bay Trail

Hiking   Strenuous   2 hours   6.4 km

The trail follows an abandoned logging road to Sawyer Bay. There are a number of hills to provide you with views of the park, and wild berries are abundant in season.

Sifting Lake Trail

Hiking   Moderate   2 hours   2 km

This .5-m-wide earth path is a linear trail and takes you to the shores of Sifting Lake. The trail is not well maintained.

Talus Lake Trail

Hiking   Strenuous   2.5 hours   5 km

This linear trail takes you past three secluded lakes, a sedge meadow, spectacular cliffs, talus (scree) slopes and a small waterfall. The trail is also known for its wildlife.

Twin Pine Lake Trail

Hiking   Strenuous   2.5 hours   4.7 km

This linear trail joins the Burma and Kabeyun Trails, and passes Twinpine Lake. Use caution, as this trail goes from lake to coast and can be very wet, making walking difficult.

Sea Lion Trail

Hiking   Easy   30 minutes   1 km (return)

This linear trail is reached only from the Kabeyun Trail. It takes you to an impressive landform known as the Sea Lion. Jutting out into Lake Superior, this rock formation is part of the Sleeping Giant legend.

Middlebrun Bay Trail

| Hiking | Easy | 2 hours | 4.2 km |
| Backpacking | | | |

This linear trail leads to Finlay Bay on Lake Superior, where there is a sandy beach. Nearby is a fen, a wetland produced by a non-acidic environment.

Pickerel Lake Trail

| Hiking | Moderate | 3–4 hours | 10 km |

This linear trail leads you through an impressive white pine stand. You can join this trail at a number of points.

The Chimney Trail*

| Hiking | Very strenuous | 3–4 hours | 9 km |
| Backpacking | | | |

This linear trail starts at the South Kabeyun trailhead. There is a 250-m climb to the top of the Sleeping Giant, and the panorama is breathtaking. From atop the highest cliff in Ontario, the Sibley Peninsula, Lake Superior and its north shore, as well as Thunder Cape are all visible. A note of caution: do not attempt this climb in wet weather.

*Al's Picks, see page 47.

AL'S PICKS

Blue Lake Provincial Park: The Spruce Fen Trail

This popular trail takes you into a world that is both interesting and very unusual, the world of the fen. Ideal for a family outing, this short, barrier-free boardwalk takes you through a succession of plant communities which are dependent on the availability of water. As you walk through this wetland community, you may not realize you are walking on a floating mat of water-logged mosses and peat, supporting a limited diversity of plants. The plants that do exist in this wet desert are the strongest of the strong, able to withstand a low nutrient supply, high acidity and lack of water.

How does a wetland resemble a desert? If you take a look at the most common shrub in the fen, Labrador tea, your question will be answered. Labrador tea has similar characteristics to plants found in the hot sand desert. It lessens water evaporation with waxy, leathery leaves that curl under, and with an undercoat of white to orange hairs. Using the information outlined on the interpretive displays, examine the other plants in the fen environment, such as leatherleaf, bog cranberry, snowberry and bog rosemary, to see other desert plant similarities.

As you walk on down the boardwalk, you will see open water where the wetland changes to an open fen. There is a visible line where the black spruce trees and Labrador tea shrubs stop and the cotton grass and carnivorous plants of the fen begin.

These plants have evolved to survive in a low-nutrient environment. A good pair of eyes will spot a red carpet of sparkling red, jewel-like plants — the sundews. With a hand lens, you can examine the sundew's sticky tentacles, which it uses to capture its prey. Further along the trail you may see a pitcher plant. This plant traps and consumes insects in leaves which are cleverly formed to resemble a pitcher for the unsuspecting insect to drink from. (Don't step off the boardwalk or you may have a close encounter with a meat-eating plant!)

Leave the open fen, and you enter a world shaded by the heavy tops of black spruce trees. The atmosphere of this forest is enhanced by the presence of "ghosts." If you see a white plant looking like a pipe, you have met the phantom of the black spruce forest. This is the Indian pipe, or ghost plant, and it has adapted to the lack of sunlight. It does not use chlorophyll but lives on decaying plant matter.

In direct contrast to the damp wetland of the fen, the trail now enters the dry upland of a jack pine forest. Here the plant community is supported by nutrients from rainwater. As you follow the trail, you will see evidence of the nutrients carried by rain, supporting a lush plant life far more diverse than the one you just left behind. Ahead is the trailhead.

Kakabeka Falls Provincial Park: Mountain Portage Walking Trail

Starting from the parking lot near the information centre, this short, flat and barrier-free looped trail combines a walk along a historic trail used by native peoples, explorers, traders, soldiers and settlers. The return route is along the top of a scenic gorge, 39 m deep, cut by the Kakabeka Falls as they erode the rocks of the Kaministiquia River.

Our walk starts away from the river using a route carved out by voyageurs in the 1870s.

Travelling through a windy area of black spruce, poplar and hemlock with dense trailside vegetation, to the sounds of the falls, it is not difficult to imagine what it must have been like for the native peoples, explorers or troops carrying supplies, canoes and equipment over the Mountain Portage.

On your right, about midway down the trail, the original Mountain Portage leads down a steep slope into a more wooded area, and on to the river below.

This section of the trail is referred to as the Little Falls Trail. The route meanders along the riverbank, then follows a creek to a waterfall. Trail markers are located en route, and the main barrier-free Mountain Portage Trail continues straight ahead.

The return portion of the trail weaves along the lip of the narrow, steep-walled rock gorge of the Kaministiquia River. The trail follows the edge of the steep cliffs in places, and viewing pods extend out beyond the cliffs, providing spectacular views of the river below. Directly opposite the last viewing pod there is a cavity in the rock, which, according to legend, is the residence of a malevolent spirit.

Just before leaving the trail, take a moment for a last view of the Kakabeka Falls ("kah-kah-pee-kah," or "thundering water," in Ojibwa). The falls are often shrouded in a light mist. No wonder many people call them Little Niagara.

Neys Provincial Park: Under the Volcano Trail

The name of this trail is intriguing, and the starting point at Prisoner's Cove adds interest to the anticipated hike. During the Second World War the government of Canada constructed a prisoner-of-war camp here. Little security was required as the impenetrable wilderness of Lake Superior's north shore formed a natural barrier. Very little remains of the camp today but park heritage interpreters have many stories about life in the camp from first-hand accounts of former prisoners and guards.

This is an easy walk for the whole family. The Point Hiking Trail, which originates at the Prisoner's Cove picnic area, connects to the Under the Volcano Trail, creating a 2.5-km linear trail. From the parking lot, you cross a small bridge onto a narrow path travelling through a black spruce forest. Long, grey old man's beard lichen hangs from the black trunks of the spruce trees, and dark green moss provides a carpet beneath your feet. A peaceful walk, especially in the early morning sunlight.

This is a short section, and you soon leave the forest behind for an open sandy beach.

Here, woodchips from the local mill have washed up on the shore and you will find yourself walking no longer on sand, but on woodchips. About 20 minutes later, the trail leaves the beach and enters a small, forested area. Walking along an earth path you can hear the waves from Lake Superior crashing on the rocks. Coming out of the forest you will see two large abandoned fishing boats. Two interpretive panels erected near the boats explain their historical significance. Just ten paces to the west of these boats the Under the Volcano Trail starts, and the adventure begins.

It takes about an hour to walk. Allow yourself enough time to read all 14 interpretive displays and learn this fascinating geological story. There are no trail markers, and you travel from one interpretive panel to the next as they zigzag along the shoreline. Most of the walk is over smooth, flat rock, but there are portions of the route that cross over rock boulder fields. Sturdy footwear is recommended, and caution exercised if you climb over the wet rocks.

As you explore the relatively flat rocky trail, imagine yourself walking back in to time and into the magma chamber of an active volcano. At the third interpretive display excellent graphics illustrate just where inside the volcano you are standing.

It is surprising to discover that the cooling of this magma produced one of the largest collections of volcanic, alkaline rock in North America. The rock contains high levels of elements such as sodium and potassium, and the colours are striking: grey nepheline, black amphiboles, bright red natrolite and pink alkali feldspar are all found in long grooves in the rock.

Be prepared to see rock ghosts, black invaders and gabbros! All are colourfully described on the interpretive display panels. As you walk further, there are long, uninterrupted views both north and south along the shores of Lake Superior. Its stark beauty and turbulent waters were made legendary by the painters of the Group of Seven. Lawren Harris's Pic Island is clearly visible from the trail, and the rocky wilderness they captured on canvas is all around you.

By the time you have reached the last interpretive display, number 14, you will have walked for an hour and learned much about Ontario's volcanoes. If you have paused to enjoy the scenery, rested on the rocks or taken some photos, you will probably have been on the trail for at least two hours. Retracing your steps to the start of the trail is a little quicker, but not disappointing. The knowledge you have gained from the display panels makes the return over the rocks even more enjoyable. What were just marks in the stone now make you stop to look at ghosts and gabbros. The lake and its islands look different. Maybe it's the change of view and light, or maybe it's because you have slowed down to enjoy all the aspects of this unique trail.

Sleeping Giant Provincial Park: The Chimney Trail

Across the water from Thunder Bay lies the profile of a giant, his arms folded across his chest, and head, legs and knees clearly visible from the shoreline. This is Sleeping Giant Provincial Park, and the Chimney Trail will take you to the knees of the Giant. It is both challenging and very rewarding for the adventurous hiker.

In the Ojibwa legend of the Sleeping Giant, the giant, Nanabosho, led the Ojibwa people to the north shore of Lake Superior to escape their enemies, the Sioux. One day, Nanabosho scratched a rock and discovered silver. Although he considered it worthless to the Ojibwa, Nanabosho buried the silver in a tiny islet off the Sibley Peninsula, because he knew that if the white men found it they would take the Ojibwa's island from them.

Although sworn to secrecy, a chieftain boasted of the silver and one day Nanabosho saw a Sioux warrior canoeing across the lake leading two white men to the hoard of silver. Nanabosho disobeyed the Great Spirit, raised a storm, and sank the canoe. As punishment for his actions the Great Spirit turned Nanabosho to stone, where he lies on his back to this day.

This is just one of many legends associated with this area. Unlike other trails highlighted in this guide, the Chimney Trail is specifically designed for the hiker who wants a physically demanding hiking experience, with an added adrenaline rush! The Chimney is extremely rugged and should only be attempted by those in excellent physical condition. It is strongly recommended that you climb with a partner. An alternative route is the Chest Trail, which climbs the Giant using a less challenging, but still strenuous route. Hikers climb to the Giant's chest with a view over his head towards the city of Thunder Bay. Consult with park officials before attempting any of these routes. Climbing in wet weather is not recommended.

The 16-km Chimney Trail is a gruelling climb to the knees of the Giant. You start at the Kabeyun Trail parking lot, and after two hours of the wide, easy and well-marked Kabeyun Trail, you come to the shores of Tea Harbour. Up ahead are the vertical faces of the Chimney, the highest vertical cliffs in Ontario. You are now at the halfway point of your hike.

At a junction, you turn right and follow the well-marked, linear Chimney Trail towards the base of the massive talus cliff. Reaching the base, you start by climbing up, over and around huge boulders. Park officials have painted blue spots on both sides of the boulders, making the route in both directions easy to find. As you ascend the talus slope, be careful as there is no designated path. Watch for loose rock material and, whether travelling with your partner or as part of a group, be sure to stay close to each other. Loosened or falling rock material will not have gained momentum, giving the downslope hiker time to react. After about one hour, take a minute to rest, check progress and enjoy the view of Lehtinen's Bay.

When you reach the base of the cliff you still have about another hour of climbing. Looking up, you will see a rock seam that opens up along the cliff. This is the "chimney" — a seam of hard granite about 3 m wide, which will serve as your path to the top. This path is extremely steep. It is almost vertical, but there are various handholds and footholds along the way. Take your time, keep going and you will succeed in reaching the top.

Emerging from the chimney, you will be tired but triumphant. Now you enter a small forest of poplar, alder and conifer. How did it get up here, at 244 m? And there are even tracks of moose and signs of beaver. Coming out of the forest, you are finally rewarded. The views are breathtaking. As you look out over Lake Superior, with the wind whipping around you, the waves crashing far below, and the expanse of wide open sky above, you truly feel on top of the world. The city of Thunder Bay, Silver Islet and Isle Royale National Park in the United States are all in clear view. Enjoy it! Eat your lunch, but remember to give yourself at least three hours of daylight to retrace your steps.

NORTHEASTERN REGION

PARKS OF THE REGION

Esker Lakes
Fushimi Lake
Greenwater
Ivanhoe Lake
Kap-Kig-Iwan
Kettle Lakes

Lake Superior
Nagagamisis
Obatanga
Pancake Bay
Potholes
Rene Brunelle

The Shoals
Tidewater
Wakami Lake
White Lake

ESKER LAKES PROVINCIAL PARK

Box 129, Swastika, Ontario P0K 1T0

Information: Call 705 568-7677
Fax 705 642-9715

Operating season: May to September

Location: The park is 37 km northeast of Kirkland Lake off Highway 672.

Natural features: Twenty-nine kettle lakes, one of the largest eskers in Ontario, sand dunes, and other post-glacial formations can be seen from the trails. The park is perched on top of a continental divide known as the Arctic Watershed. Rain on the south side flows to the Atlantic and rain on the north side flows to James Bay. Fires in the 1950s caused large, burnt-over patches where jack pine and white birch now thrive.

All the trails are looped, 0.5 m wide, travelling over an earth path with boardwalk sections. A French and English trail guide is available for Lonesome Bog. Conducted nature walks are offered and a mountain-biking trail is available.

Lonesome Bog Trail

Interpretive guide   Easy   1 hour   1.2 km

Trail users will walk through a spruce bog, where insectivorous plants may be seen, and on a section of the longest esker in Ontario. There are nine interpretive stops explaining bog vegetation.

Trapper's Trail*

Hiking/Map   Moderate   3 hours   9 km

The trail crosses over the longest esker in Ontario and passes an old Trapper's cabin. There is one maintained loop of 9 km with plans to have two other loops (13 km and 21 km) further developed.

*Al's Picks, see page 68.

FUSHIMI LAKE PROVINCIAL PARK
Box 670, Hearst, Ontario P0L 1N0

Information: Call 705 362-4164
705 362-4346
Fax 705 362 -7515

Operating season: May to September

Location: The park is situated near Highway 11, about 41 km northwest of Hearst.

Natural features: Fushimi Lake is ringed by a band of eastern white cedar, which in turn is surrounded by a dense, boreal forest, dominated by spruce, balsam, poplar and birch. The narrow band of cedar around the shoreline is broken by several large rocky outcrops, and at the mouth of the Valentine River there is a stand of exceptionally large tamaracks. Smaller plants in the park include stemless lady's slipper and Indian pipe.

Both of the park's trails are linear, 0.5 m wide, and follow earth paths.

Fire Tower Trail

Hiking   Strenuous   2.5 hours   3.5 km (return)

The trail takes you to one of the few fire towers left standing in the province. Also, there is an abandoned ranger's cabin at the base of the fire tower.

Achilles' Lake Trail

Hiking   Easy   45 minutes   2 km (return)

After travelling through a boreal forest you come to the shores of Achilles' Lake.

GREENWATER PROVINCIAL PARK
Box 730, Cochrane, Ontario P0L 1C0

Information: Call 705 272-6335
             Fax   705 336-2983

Operating season: May to September

Location: About 14 km north of Highway 11, 32 km northwest of Cochrane.

Natural features: The park's two significant land formations, eskers and kettles, were formed after the glaciers retreated. The eskers were formed in tunnels left by melt-water flowing under the decaying ice. Sand and gravel eventually filled those tunnels which became steep-sided ridges called eskers. The park has one 60-m-high esker.

Several of the park's 26 lakes are kettle lakes, formed when large blocks of ice were buried by the collapse of overlying sediments that delayed the melting action. The ice made deep depressions in the sandy soil which later filled with water as the ice melted, forming small lakes. Their green colour gives the park its name.

The trail can be used for snowshoeing.

Green Trail

Interpretive guide   Moderate   45 minutes   1 km

This loop is 1.0 m wide, travelling over an earth path with a few steep climbs. There are nine interpretive stops. The guide quizzes hikers' knowledge of plants and trees.

IVANHOE LAKE PROVINCIAL PARK

190 Cherry Street, Chapleau, Ontario P0M 1K0

Information: Call 705 899-2644
                       705 864-1710
               Fax 705 899-2778

Operating season: May to September

Location: South of Highway 101, halfway between Chapleau and Timmins.

Natural features: A special feature of the park is an unusual "quaking bog" — an old kettle lake overgrown with vegetation. Over the centuries, the plants covering the water have created a floating mat. Visible from one of the nature trails, this unusual bog shimmies and shakes when disturbed.

There are unusual plants in and near the park, including six varieties of orchid. Opportunities for seeing wildlife such as moose and osprey are common.

The three trails are looped, a minimum of 1.5 m wide, and travel primarily over an earth path with some boardwalk sections. Conducted nature walks are offered.

Saw Lake Trail

Interpretive displays Easy   1.5 hours   3 km

The route takes you over an esker ridge past active beaver lodges and along the Saw Lake shoreline. Interpretive panels explain the glacial formation of this area.

Teck Lake Trail

Hiking   Moderate   1 hour   1.6 km

The trail offers solitude to those who venture through a mature boreal forest to the shores of peaceful Teck Lake. There are a few steep grades.

Quaking Bog Trail

Interpretive displays Easy   30 minutes   0.8km

Trail users walk over ground that was once the bottom of Ivanhoe Lake. Interpretive panels at the viewing platform explain the unique quaking bog.

KAP-KIG-IWAN

Box 129, Swastika, Ontario P0K 1T0

Operating season: May to September

Information: Call 705 544-2050 (May to September)
                    705 544-8075 (October to April)
              Fax 705 544-8737

Location: Near Highway 11, 2 km south of the town of Englehart, between New Liskeard and Kirkland Lake.

Natural features: The main feature of the park is the fast-flowing Englehart River, with a waterfall, several series of whitewater rapids, rugged rock outcrops and deep ravines. The park's waterfalls, mixed forests and colourful flowers provide excellent opportunities for photographs.

The erosive action of the river has exposed more than two billion years of Earth's geology, visible in the walls and floors of the river valley. The lowest layers are among the oldest rocks in the world. An intermediate level contains fossilized records of early life forms, and the layers toward the top show the effects of the last Ice Age.

All trails are about 1.0 m wide, travelling mostly over an earth path. The Upper Circle trail is available for crossing country skiing.

Hell's Gate Trail

Hiking   Moderate   1 hour   2.5 km (return)

This linear trail follows the riverbank past several sets of rushing rapids. During spring runoff the waterfall is spectacular.

Cedar Trail

Hiking   Easy   2 hours   4.5 km

The trail is named for a 150-year-old cedar that withstood a major forest fire in 1922. It is located near the end of the trail. Trail users see a beaver lodge and enjoy a scenic view from a lookout overlooking the river before looping back to the start of the trail.

Upland Circle Trail

| Hiking | Moderate | 2.5 hours | 5 km |

This wilderness, looped trail is excellent for birdwatching. It travels through stands of pine, beech and poplar.

KETTLE LAKES PROVINCIAL PARK

896 Riverside Drive, Timmins, Ontario P4N 3W2

Information: Call 705 363-3511
  Fax 705 360-2022

Operating season: May to October
  December to March

Location: The park is 40 km east of Timmins via Highway 67 off Highway 101.

Natural features: There are 20 glacially formed kettle lakes in the park. These lakes have no inlets or outlets; their water comes from springs. The park is located in the transition zone between boreal forest and sub-arctic tundra. The forest cover is jack pine, trembling aspen and white birch growing on very dry sites. Pink lady's slipper, bush honeysuckle, yellow clintonia and pitcher plants are readily found in this park.

All the trails are looped, 1.0 m wide, and on earth paths. Conducted nature walks are offered and there are cross-country ski and snowshoeing trails.

Oh-Say-Yah-Wuh-Kaw Trail

| Interpretive displays | Moderate | 1 hour | 2 km |

There are four interpretive displays about the events that shaped the park. In particular, geological features such as erratics and eskers are discussed.

Kettle Trail

| Interpretive guide | Moderate | 1 hour | 2 km |

Circling a typical kettle lake, the trail has ten interpretive stops which explain the unique vegetation growing near the trail.

Tamarack Trail

| Hiking | Moderate | 1 hour | 1.5 km |

This trail travels through a boreal forest and around a black spruce bog.

Wintergreen Trail

| Hiking | Moderate | 1 hour | 1.5 km |

The ground along the trail is covered with an abundance of wintergreen plants, and you will be walking mainly through a forested area of jack pine and trembling aspen.

LAKE SUPERIOR PROVINCIAL PARK

Box 267, Wawa, Ontario P0S 1K0

Information: Call 705 856-2284
Fax 705 856-1333

Operating season: May to October

Location: The park is located on Highway 17, on the eastern shore of Lake Superior, south of Wawa, and north of Sault Ste. Marie.

Natural features: The park's high, rounded hills are remnants of ancient mountain ranges, worn down over eons by glaciers. Rushing rivers drop rapidly from the interior highlands to the Lake Superior shoreline, creating rapids and dramatic waterfalls. Steep-walled valleys with granite and gneiss provide some of Ontario's most beautiful scenery especially in the autumn when the brilliant colours of the southern deciduous trees contrast with the dark green boreal conifers.

The park has moose, timber wolf, Canada lynx and bears, while smaller mammals include red fox, red squirrel, beaver and marten. Woodland caribou, reintroduced to the park in the 1980s, are seen occasionally. More than 250 species of bird have been identified inside the park, and 120 species nest here.

All the trails are about 0.5 m wide, travelling primarily over an earth and rock surface. Seven of the ten trails are looped. Conducted nature walks are offered. The trail guides are available in French and English.

Agawa Rock Indian Pictographs Trail

Interpretive displays   Moderate   30 minutes   0.4 km

This internationally renowned sacred pictograph site is one of a few in Ontario that is accessible by trail. The linear trail is one metre in width with a surface of smooth rock and earth. There are two large signs explaining the native pictographs. To see them you descend a stone stairway for approximately 15 m to a 2-m-wide ledge along Lake Superior. Caution is advised when venturing onto this rock ledge due to its slope and the unpredictable nature of Lake Superior's waters. The rewards are seeing the pictographs close-up, and getting unrestricted views of the lake and nearby islands. Steep cliffs line one side of the trail, which runs to the rock paintings on a 30-m-high shoreline bluff.

Coastal Trail

Backpacking   Strenuous   5–7 days   60 km
Map

The winding linear route of this trail traces the rugged coastline along cliffs, sand beaches, cobble beaches, and sculpted black rocks. At Gargantua Harbour there are cobbles the size of melons. Deep-blue harebells nestle in spaces between the rocks. Arctic-alpine plants such as butterwort and encrusted saxifrage are found along the coast on outcrops of rock. Look for bald eagles and double-crested cormorants, especially between the Sand and Agawa Rivers. Sections of the trail may be hiked in shorter day trips.

Caution: This is a rugged area and can be very slippery when wet due to lichen on the rocks.

Nokomis Trail

Hiking   Moderate   1.5–3 hours   5 km

The trail takes you through a stand of boreal forest to emerge with spectacular views of Lake Superior. At the first lookout, the transition between the Great Lakes–St. Lawrence environment and boreal forests is evident. At the last lookout a craggy rock formation resembling an old woman's face may be seen in the cliff to the west. This formation gave Old Woman's Bay its name.

Peat Mountain Trail

| Hiking | Strenuous | 3–5 hours | 11 km |

This route includes a number of lookout sites, from which there are panoramic views of the park's glacier, moulded, rolling hills and the Old Woman River. The trail is particularly noted for its spring flowers and bright fall colours.

Trapper's Trail

| Hiking | Easy | 1 hour | 1.5 km |

This former trapline trail is looped, with a variety of surfaces, including gravel, floating boardwalk and earth path. It follows the shoreline of Rustle Lake and takes you through a wetland area. There are two viewing platforms. Moose may be seen from the bog lake boardwalk and platforms at dawn or dusk. Observers may catch a glimpse of river otter, marten, flycatchers and black-backed woodpecker or see signs of beaver activity.

South Old Woman River Trail

| Hiking | Moderate | 2 hours | 2.5 km |

The trail takes you through a damp forest by the side of a river which nurtures a diversity of ferns and wildflowers. A good location to look for boreal forest birds.

Orphan Lake Trail*

| Hiking | Moderate | 3.5 hours | 8 km |

You will walk through many habitats on this trail, including lake and river shores. There is a shift from southern Great Lakes–St. Lawrence forest to northern boreal forest as the trail descends to the lake. In the hardwoods, look for spring wildflowers, and listen for black-throated blue warblers and scarlet tanager. Be sure to bring your bird book and keep the warbler page open! On the way down to the lake, watch for bay-breasted and Cape May warblers among the spruce, and you may see northern parula. The trail follows the shoreline to the Baldhead River, where visitors can stop and enjoy the series of rapids and waterfalls.

*Al's Picks, see page 69.

Awausee Trail

| Hiking | Strenuous | 4–6 hours | 10 km |

Walking through a forested valley carved by glacial meltwater, hikers will notice that the river was much larger at one time. A series of terraces created by various river levels is evidence of this. There are four lookouts that provide spectacular views of the Agawa Valley. Spring flowers, migrating birds and fall colours are highlights of this trail. A portion of the trail (to the first lookout and back to the trailhead) can be hiked in 45 minutes.

Towab Trail

| Backpacking Map | Very strenuous | 2–3 days | 24 km (return) |

This linear trail follows the valley of the Agawa River to 25-m-high Agawa Falls. Spectacular scenery is complemented by spring wildflowers and colourful fall leaves. In season, the salmon migration makes this an exciting trail. Watch for bald eagles and osprey, especially in the spring and fall.

Pinguisibi Trail

| Interpretive displays | Easy | 2.5 hours | 6 km (return) |

This trail is popular with anglers in the spring and with picnickers and hikers during the summer months. It is linear and runs over rock, boardwalk and earth path past a series of rapids and waterfalls. This was an ancient Ojibwa travel route, and there are seven interpretive display panels explaining the importance of the river to the Ojibwa for food and travel.

Crescent Lake

| Hiking | Easy | 1 hour | 2 km (return) |

This is an ideal family hike. The trail travels through a mature Great Lakes–St. Lawrence hardwood forest where yellow birch are at least 80 years old and the great pines dominating the forest have been here for over a century. Hikers pass by a number of lakes.

NAGAGAMISIS PROVINCIAL PARK

Box 670, Hearst, Ontario P0L 1N0

Information: Call 807 868-2254
Fax 705 362-7515

Operating season: May to September

Location: The park is located on Highway 631 about 30 km north of Hornepayne, 42 km south of Highway 11.

Natural features: Nagagamisis is a Cree word meaning "lake with fine, sandy shores." This park, which lies on a narrow peninsula, owes the sandiness of its shores to the retreating glacier. In addition, clusters of small, irregular moraines, kames, and other glacial features are found throughout the park.

Reminders of former human activity include the remains of a trapper's cabin, two Ojibwa graveyards, and pottery fragments indicating that nomads lived in the area for at least 1,000 years.

Both trails are looped, 0.5 m wide, and have earth surfaces.

Time Trail

Interpretive guide   Moderate   1.5 hours   3 km

The trail travels through a boreal forest. It has 12 interpretive stops that discuss features such as beaver dams and the geology of the area.

Shaganash Trail

Interpretive guide   Moderate   2 hours   4 km

The route follows the shoreline of Nagagamisis Lake. There are 12 interpretive stops. The guide explains how the Cree and Ojibwa made use of the native plants and animals to survive in this environment

OBATANGA PROVINCIAL PARK

Box 340, White River, Ontario P0M 3G0

Information   Call 807 822-2592 (summer only)
              Fax   807 822-2592 (summer only)

Operating season: early June to mid-September

Location: The park is 55 km west of Wawa and 35 km east of White River on Highway 17.

Natural features: The forests are a result of fires in the early 1900s. The predominant tree species is jack pine, which requires fire to seed successfully. Other vegetation is typical of a boreal forest: black spruce wetlands and white birch and balsam fir in upland areas. A wide variety of wildflowers such as the moccasin flower can be found growing next to the trail.

The trail guide is available in both French and English. Conducted nature walks are offered.

Forest Fire Trail

Interpretive guide   Easy   1.5 hours   2.4 km

This looped, 0.5-m-wide earth path travels through a boreal forest of jack pine and black spruce. There are 11 interpretive stops that discuss forest fire ecology and what happens during and after a forest fire.

PANCAKE BAY PROVINCIAL PARK

Box 61, Batchawana Bay, Ontario P0S 1A0

Information: Call 705 882-2209
              Fax   705 882-2124

Operating season: May to October

Location: The park lies along the Lake Superior shoreline on Highway 17, about 76 km north of Sault Ste. Marie.

Natural features: There is a beach of fine, pure sand, about 3 km in length. It is sheltered from the open lake by the two protective cliffs that form the bay. Pine trees are most common along the shoreline, while further inland, yellow birch and sugar maples predominate and stunted cedars grow in the wetlands. Wild strawberries, raspberries, blueberries and cranberries, as well as hazelnuts are abundant. Wildlife includes chipmunks, beavers, muskrats, squirrels and several species of bird.

All the trails are looped, a minimum of 0.5 m wide, and travel over sand and earth surfaces. A combined trail guide and map is available in both French and English.

Pancake Trail

Interpretive displays   Easy   2 hours   3.5 km

This fairly level trail has 12 interpretive stops that help track the impact of humankind on the local environment. Some sections of the trail have boardwalks, which allow access to the Black Bog.

Pancake Bay Hiking Trail

Hiking   Moderate   4–6 hours   12 km

The trail leads to a viewing lookout tower and a series of waterfalls on the Pancake River.

POTHOLES PROVINCIAL PARK
190 Cherry Street , Chapleau, Ontario P0M 1K0

Information: Call 705 864-1710
             Fax 705 899-2778

Operating season: June to September

Location: The park is on Highway 101, about 35 km east of Wawa.

Natural features: A complex of glacial potholes and troughs in the Kinniwabi River gives the nature reserve its name. Sedges and fronds grow along the riverbanks, while jack pines and blueberry bushes predominate in the forest.

Potholes Trail

Interpretive displays   Easy   45 minutes   1 km

This linear, 1.0 m wide earth path and boardwalk trail travels to a bridge across the river where you are able to get a clear view of the potholes. A series of interpretive panels explain how these potholes were formed.

RENE BRUNELLE PROVINCIAL PARK

6 Government Road, Kapuskasing, Ontario P5N 2W4

Information: Call 705 367-2692
                Fax 705 367-2725

Operating season: May to September

Location: The park is north of Highway 11, 13 km from the town of Moonbeam. It is 32 km east of Kapuskasing, on the east side of Remi Lake.

Natural features: This park is located in what geologists call the Great Clay Belt, an island of deep, fertile soil set in the midst of the rocky Canadian Shield. Thousands of years ago, a glacial lake covered the area. It left deposits of silt and clay sediment which foster an unusual medley of environments. These include an extensive warm water lake, some of the best beaches in the region and a rich and varied forest community.

Both trails are looped, 1.0 m wide, and travel over earth path and boardwalk surfaces. There are two cross-country ski trails.

La Vigilance Trail

Interpretive displays   Easy   1 hour   1.5 km

There are three display panels with information about early aviation at Remi Lake.

Spruce Lowland Trail

Interpretive guide   Easy   1 hour   1.6 km

There are five interpretive stops. Each explains one aspect of plant and tree life found in a boreal forest.

THE SHOALS PROVINCIAL PARK
190 Cherry Street, Chapleau, Ontario P0M 1K0

Information: Call 705 864-1160
            Fax 705 899-2778

Operating season: June to September

Location: The park is 48 km west of Chapleau, off Highway 101.

Natural features: Eskers — long, sinuous ridges of sand and gravel that were once the beds of ancient rivers — are found in many regions of Ontario. Two eskers form the shoals in Little Wawa Lake, and lend their name to the park. There are 28 distinct plant communities, including coniferous forest, herbaceous wetland and marsh.

Moose, timber wolf, red fox, beaver and otter are residents of the park. It is also a haven for birds, among them osprey, great blue heron and several species of hawk and owl.

The Lonesome Bog Trail

Interpretive displays Easy   1 hour   1 km

This 1.0-m-wide, looped earth-and-boardwalk trail takes you to a black spruce bog. There are two interpretive panels along the path that discuss the ecology of a black spruce forest, and its plants and animals. An interpretive display panel located on the boardwalk explains the life of a bog. It is common to see a variety of wildlife in this area.

TIDEWATER PROVINCIAL PARK
Box 730, Cochrane, Ontario P0L 1C0

Information: Call 705 336-2987
Fax 705 272-7183

Operating season: June to September

Location: The park is located at the mouth of the Moose River, near the town of Moosonee on James Bay. Access is by watercraft only.

Natural features: Situated just 20 km from the salt waters of James Bay, the park consists of four islands in the Moose River. Here the Arctic tides rise and fall twice daily, varying as much as 2.5 m from high to low.

The vegetation is stunted and less dense because of the northerly latitude and proximity to the tree line. Tamarack, black and white spruce and balsam poplar grow along the shores of the islands. Cranberries, raspberries, willow, laurel and calypso orchid are all common in the area. Seals and beluga whales may occasionally be seen in the Moose River.

Access to the park is by water taxi available from the boat docks in Moosonee and Moose Factory.

Riverside Trail

Interpretive guide   Easy   1 hour   2 km

This looped trail is 1.0 m wide, travelling on an earth path. There are 14 interpretive stops describing the formation of the island and the specialized trees and plants that grow here.

WAKAMI LAKE PROVINCIAL PARK
190 Cherry Street, Chapleau, Ontario P0M 1K0

Information: Call 705 233-2853
Fax 705-233-2853

Operating season: May to September

Location: The park is located 60 km southeast of Chapleau. On Highway 129 southeast from Chapleau turn east on Highway 667 for 30 km.

Natural features: The park is situated along the height of land between the Atlantic and Arctic watersheds. As a result there are two distinct sections in the park: the southern section with tree species such as sugar maple and white pine that are characteristic of the Great Lakes–St. Lawrence forest, and the northern section with boreal forest species such as jack pine and northern fir. This division between forest types is very noticeable.

Wildlife such as chipmunks, squirrels, and hares, as well as spring peeper, blue-spotted salamander and several varieties of frog are often seen, as are birds such as bald eagle, pileated woodpecker and various species of owl.

Most of the trails are loops, 1.5 m wide, travelling over an earth path with some boardwalk sections. Some trails provide both English and French displays and/or guidebooks. Conducted nature walks are offered.

Hidden Bog Trail

Hiking   Moderate   2.5 hours   7 km

This linear trail travels over an earth path, bridge and boardwalk to a sphagnum bog. There are some steep climbs.

Historic Logging Exhibit Trail

Interpretive guide   Easy   45 minutes   1 km

Restored logging equipment and buildings are displayed along the trail. There are French and English interpretive panels and a trail guide explaining the history of logging in the area.

Transitional Forest Trail

Hiking   Moderate   2 hours   5 km

Walking through this area you will experience the transition from southern Ontario tree species (Great Lakes–St. Lawrence) vegetation to northern (boreal) forest species. There is an optional second loop which adds 2 km and 45 minutes to the trail.

Beaver Meadow Discovery Trail

Interpretive guide	Easy	1.5 hours	2.5 km

You walk beneath jack pines encircling an abandoned beaver pond. The guide describes the effects of beavers on a section of boreal forest.

Height of Land Trail

Backcountry Map	Strenuous	5–6 days	76 km

Running through primarily boreal forests, the trail follows the watershed, or height of land, which separates the flow of waters to north and south. Good views, the opportunity to observe wildlife, and isolation are its main features.

WHITE LAKE PROVINCIAL PARK

Box 340, White River, Ontario P0M 3G0

Information: Call 807 822-2447 (Park)
            Fax 807 822-2621

Operating season: Early May to late September

Location: The park is located 35 km west of White River and 60 km east of Marathon on Highway 17.

Natural features: The park lies within the rugged Canadian Shield in a sandy basin containing several small lakes and bogs. Metamorphic bedrock outcrops are found in a few areas of the park. The boreal forest is well represented in the park by the variety of shrubs, mosses and wildflowers, including several species of orchid.

All the trails are 0.5 m wide, travelling over an earth path with some boardwalk sections. Conducted nature walks are offered, and French and English trail guides are available. The park has a specially marked fitness trail.

Deer Lake Trail

Interpretive display	Easy	1–2 hours	1.5 or 2.5 km

The trail has two loops and there are a few steep climbs. The first loop has six interpretive stops, the second, nine. They discuss tree species such as black spruce and cedar, and throughout the walk the beaver and its role in this environment is described in detail. The trail travels through a pine forest and follows the shore of Deer Lake and Beaver Marsh. The first loop ends at a viewing point with a bench overlooking a beaver meadow.

Tiny Bog Trail

Hiking	Moderate	2.5 hours	4.5 km

The trail loops around a spruce bog and two large beaver ponds, then ascends a sandy ridge area where the jack pine is the dominant species. A boardwalk provides access to the bog. A viewing platform and rest benches are located along the trail. Visitors may notice a number of insectivorous plants. There are some steep grades, and the walking surface is uneven with exposed roots and rocks.

Clearwater Trail

Hiking	Easy	1 hour	2 km (return)

This linear trail travels to the beautiful, spring-fed waters of Clearwater Lake. It also meanders through pine forests and wildflowers, and passes by two small lakes. Clearwater Lake is filled from an underground spring and is crystal clear. A variety of wildflowers abound throughout the summer and many types of mosses and lichen carpet the forest floor.

AL'S PICKS

Eskers Lake Provincial Park: Trapper's Trail

This ancient Ojibwa route offers the hiker a chance to see kettle lakes, eskers, interesting mature forest types, scenic vistas and a historic site. An interpretive guide and map illustrate the three-tiered trail system. This trail design provides hikers with a variety of choices based on their time and endurance. For instance, in one and a half hours you can reach the trapper's cabin, or in two hours you could be walking on top of the Munroe Esker, the largest landform of its kind in Ontario, stretching some 259 km.

The hike starts from the north end of the Panagapka Lake campgrounds parking lot with a walk past Hazel Lake where large white birch trees are found, the first growth after a forest fire that ravaged the area. A short distance from the lake brings you to a 90-year-old jack pine forest. The walking is easy for the entire trail with many rest benches provided. In about 40 minutes, you will arrive at the first major trail junction. At this intersection you can decide to return to the start of the trail or continue along the rugged, undeveloped main trail.

If you return, the trail crosses over the esker, past a mature forest of pine, and beside a kettle lake before arriving at the fire road where you turn right. Watch carefully as you walk along the old roadway for possible sightings of wolf, moose or lynx, or at least their prints in the sand.

Caution is required if you decide to continue on the main trail. The rest of the trail is poorly marked, could be flooded and has unsafe boardwalks. If you do decide to travel further, the trail will take you alongside many kettle lakes. These lakes form in the hollow or depression created by the melting of huge isolated blocks of glacial ice. They have no inlets or outlets, yet the water is clean and crystal clear.

Soon you arrive at the historic trapper's cabin just off to the left side of the trail on a sandy ridge. After exploring the cabin you continue to walk north through a magnificent forest of spruce and pine. Twenty minutes later the trail runs along the top of the Munroe esker for a short distance — the only portion of the trail built on the esker. Shortly after, you reach the second trail junction. If you are starting to feel tired, turn right to return. The trail travels past an extensive spruce bog surrounded by black spruce and tamarack trees. If you are still full of energy, you may want to take a detour to the water's edge of this bog to get a close up view of Labrador tea, sundew and pitcher plants found growing vigorously through the sphagnum moss.

Leaving the bog behind, you soon reach the fire road. Turn right and you will return to the trailhead within an hour. As you walk back keep a close eye along the sides of the roadway for the abundance of wild berry plants.

If you decide to complete the third and last loop of the trail, you will be taken to a world of solitude in a more remote part of the park. Eventually, the trail re-joins the fire road. At this juncture you have a three-hour walk back to the trailhead. The park has plans to develop these loops in the near future. Check with park staff to determine the difficulty and hazards before hiking the second and third loops.

Lake Superior Provincial Park: Orphan Lake Trail

This hike provides an excellent introduction to hiking in Lake Superior Provincial Park. It is ideal for families or for those who want to stretch their legs on a warm day without getting too hot. The trail travels through a forest, circles a lake, swings past refreshing waterfalls, and has two breathtaking lookouts with interpretive display panels explaining some of the historical and natural features of the surroundings.

The trail is very popular and as a consequence is well defined all the way. You will have no trouble at all filling most of a day with activities such as picnicking, resting and catching a few sun rays on the flat rocks near the falls, poking about among the driftwood and the great variety of colourful pebbles that accumulate along the shore of Lake Superior.

You will start your walk through a mature hardwood forest of yellow birch and sugar maple with a variety of ferns. These tall trees provide spectacular fall colours. In the spring, the forest floor is a carpet of wildflowers such as Dutchman's breeches,

Solomon's seal, nodding trillium and twisted stalk with their bell-shaped flowers on bent or twisted stalks. In 15 minutes you reach the Orphan Lake Lookout side trail. You can choose to continue or hike the short trail to the lookout. From there you will be able to see Orphan Lake and a burned-over area on the far shore. You will also notice a change to coniferous trees like black spruce, white spruce and white birch. This change is due to the cooling affects of Lake Superior.

Walking along the main trail you pass through a 5-hectare area burned by a fire caused by humans in May 1998. Notice how the new vegetation is quickly returning. Shortly, you arrive at the second side trail leading to the Lake Superior lookout. This lookout provides you with an enjoyable view of the mouth of the Baldhead River, while the walk along the lookout ridge offers a panoramic view of Lake Superior's coast. You will have to retrace your steps to return to the main trail.

From the lookout trail, the main trail descends 100 m down a narrow path to Lake Superior and a beach of colourful pebbles. There are also some interesting wave-sculpted rocks at the south end of the beach. This is the halfway point. The beach provides a junction with and access to the Coastal Trail (22 km north to Gargantua Harbour or 30 km south to Agawa Bay). To continue along the Orphan Lake trail walk along the beach to the Baldhead River and then follow the trail upstream.

Just before the falls and approximately 200 m upstream, there are two footbridges across the Baldhead River. The Orphan Lake Trail continues along the south side of the river past the falls. Crossing the bridges links you to the Coastal Trail.

Standing at the river's edge looking upstream you can enjoy impressive views of the water as it tumbles down over rock ledges, creating a series of rapids. The trail meanders alongside the river, next to evidence of the river's power, the trunks of huge trees wedged in the rocks. You gradually climb to the east shore of Orphan Lake before rejoining the main access trail. From there, you have a short walk back to the trailhead.

NEAR NORTH REGION

PARKS OF THE REGION

Arrowhead	Halfway Lake	Restoule
Chutes	Killarney	Samuel de Champlain
Driftwood	Killbear	Six Mile Lake
Fairbank	Marten River	The Massasauga
Finlayson Point	Mikisew	Windy Lake
Grundy Lake	Mississagi	

ARROWHEAD PROVINCIAL PARK

R.R. 3, 11200 Highway 11, Huntsville, Ontario P1H 2J4

Information: Call 705 789-5105
            Fax 705 789-1610

Operating season: May to October (summer)
                 December to March (winter)

Location: The park is situated along Highway 11, a short drive north of Huntsville.

Natural features: The park is characterized by two distinct areas: the rocky upland, rugged with hardwood forest, and the sandy lowland. Growing in abundance in the shallows of Arrowhead Lake is the arrowhead plant which gives the park its name. The bright crimson cardinal flower is one of several uncommon southern plants that grow here.

There are plans to convert three of the four hiking trails to interpretive trails using display panels to explain the features of the trail. All the trails travel over an earth path surface. Three trails are looped and approximately one and a half metres in width. Conducted nature walks are offered. There are approximately 29 km of cross-country ski trails in the park, as well as opportunities for snowshoeing.

Stubb's Falls Trail*

Hiking   Easy   1 hour   2 km

The trail travels over an earth path, with wood chip and boardwalk surfaces. It passes through a sugar maple forest providing excellent wildflower viewing in the spring and birdwatching all year. The trail travels to picturesque waterfalls.

*Al's Picks, see page 90.

Homesteaders Trail

Hiking   Moderate   1.5 hours   3 km

There are several steep climbs before reaching an early homestead site. Visitors can see remnants of the original milk house, stone walls, a wagon and field boundaries.

Mayflower Trail

Hiking   Moderate   45 minutes   1 km (return)

This linear trail follows the shores of Mayflower Lake where you can see a variety of aquatic plants. There are several steep grades.

Beaver Meadow Trail

Hiking   Strenuous   3 hours   6 km

This trail takes you through an area with plenty of opportunities to observe wildlife. It eventually leads to a beaver meadow and dam.

CHUTES PROVINCIAL PARK
Box 37, Massey, Ontario P0P 1P0

Information: Call 705 865-2021
             Fax 705 865-2992

Operating season: May to September

Location: The park is located near Massey, just north of Highway 17. It's the only provincial park along the Trans-Canada Highway between Sudbury and Sault Ste. Marie.

Natural features: The rapids and waterfalls of the Aux Sables River are the highlights of this park. There are several short trails leading to the river providing excellent views.

A French/English trail guide is available. There are cross-country ski trails.

The Time Trail

Interpretive guide   Easy   1.5 hours   3 km (return)

This linear trail varies from 0.5 m to 2.0 m in width, travelling over an earth path, smooth rock and sandy surface beside the Aux Sables River to views overlooking the falls. There are 12 interpretive stops explaining the geological and plant history of the area.

DRIFTWOOD PROVINCIAL PARK

Stonecliffe, Ontario K0J 2K0

Information: Call 613 586-2553
Fax 613 586-2717

Operating season: May to September

Location: Near the Ottawa River, off Highway 17, about 40 km north of Deep River.

Natural features: Concentrations of sand and gravel, and an esker are noticeable aspects of the landscape. A forest fire burnt the southern half of the park, but already aspen, poplar jack pine and blueberry bushes are thriving.

Both trails are looped, 2 m wide, and run over earth path and smooth rock.

Oak Highland Trail

Hiking   Moderate   30 minutes   1 km

This clearly marked trail has some steep grades to climb on the way up to a viewing point overlooking the Ottawa River.

Beaver Dam Loop

Interpretive guide   Moderate   1.5 hours   2 km

This trail leads to a lookout rock with a spectacular view of the Ottawa River. Its main feature, however, is an active beaver pond, which the trail encircles. There are six interpretive stops, each describing the beavers' presence, activities and influence. There are some steep grades to climb.

FAIRBANK PROVINCIAL PARK

c/o 199 Larch Street, Suite 404, Sudbury, Ontario P3E 5P9

Information: Call 705 866-0530 (after Mid-May)
Fax 705 966-0565

Operating season: May to September

Location: The park is off Highway 17, 13 km north of Worthington on Regional Road 4, about 55 km west of Sudbury.

Natural features: The park is noted for its high concentrations of nickel and copper ore. A unique feature is the Fairbank fault — a fracture in the Earth's crust — which is visible from the park's single trail. Deciduous woodlands contain yellow birch and sugar maple bordering the lakeshore. The clear spring-fed waters make it a good place for snorkelling.

Wa-Shai-Ga-Mog Trail

Interpretive displays   Moderate   30 minutes   0.5 km

This loop trail is a 1.0-m-wide, rock and earth path with some steep grades. There are 12 interpretive display stops that explain the area's nickel and copper mining history.

FINLAYSON POINT PROVINCIAL PARK
Box 38, Temagami, Ontario P0H 2H0

Information: Call 705 569-3205
                    Fax 705 569-2886

Operating Season: May to September

Location: The park is near Temagami off Highway 11 about 96 km north of North Bay.

Natural features: The park is located on a small peninsula on Lake Temagami. Known as a gateway to the vast Temagami wilderness, and for its thousands of canoe routes, the park features large white pine, steep, rugged rock cliffs, and some sandy beaches.

Discovery Trail

This looped trail, between 1.0 m and 4 m wide, travels along an earth path, and over paved and unpaved road surfaces. There are a few steep climbs. The park map serves as a trail guide, and 14 interpretive stops describe the park's trees, plants and geology.

GRUNDY LAKE PROVINCIAL PARK

R.R. 1, Britt, Ontario P0G 1A0

Information: Call 705 383-2286
Fax 705 383-2437 (request for information only)

Operating season: May to October

Location: The park is near the junction of Highways 69 and 522, about 80 km north of Parry Sound.

Natural features: A network of small lakes and forests of majestic red and white pine, yellow birch and maple makes up the landscape of this park. Small mammals such as muskrat, raccoon, mink, fox and beaver are common sightings as well as the occasional deer and moose. More than 160 species of bird have been recorded in the park.

The trails are all looped, 1.0 m wide, and run over earth paths and smooth rocks with sections of boardwalks. Conducted nature walks are offered.

Swan Lake Trail

Interpretive guide   Easy   1 hour   1.5 km

This trail has six interpretive stops. Each stop explains the ever-changing wetlands at different viewing heights and locations, while a boardwalk allows for dry-footed passage through the marsh area. The trail leads to a 10-m-high granite lookout, with a panoramic view of Swan Lake.

Gut Lake Trail

Interpretive displays Easy   1.5 hours   2.5 km

After crossing Nisbet Creek the trail ascends to the smooth, exposed rocks of the Canadian Shield. Here visitors can see the lakes, streams and wetlands which drain into Georgian Bay via the historic French River. There are many scenic viewing points along the trail. The 18 interpretive display panels describe the geology and plant life of the area.

Beaver Dam Trail

Hiking   Moderate   2.5 hours   4 km

Walking through a dense forest and wetlands, you will eventually reach the beaver dam. These animal engineers have built a structure that controls the water levels in three lakes. Of special interest too, are heron and osprey nests that can be seen from the trail. These nests look like untidy bunches of branches in the tops of swamp-killed trees.

HALFWAY LAKE PROVINCIAL PARK
c/o 199 Larch Street, Suite 404, Sudbury, Ontario P3E 5P9

Information: Call 705 965-2702
                       705 523-8195 (out of season)
            Fax 705 965-2971 (summer)
            Fax 705 523-6598 (winter)

Operating season: May to September

Location: The park straddles Highway 144 about 90 km northwest of Sudbury.

Natural features: The park bears the after-effects of glaciation: kames, moraines and a boulder field, where massive, rounded rocks lie in a jumble. The most common trees are the jack pines, but black spruce, birch and maple thrive among them. There are a number of sphagnum bogs with plants such as small-leaved cranberry and Labrador tea, and there are thick patches of wild blueberries and raspberries.

Moose are often seen in the park, and for birdwatchers, park staff have recorded 90 species of bird, including osprey and pine warbler.

All trails are looped, 0.5 m wide, and travel over an earth path. Conducted nature walks are offered.

Osprey Heights Trail

Hiking   Strenuous   3 hours   7 km

The trail leads to a number of breathtaking views of Antrim Lake and limitless tracts of boreal forest. There are some significant grades to climb.

Moose Ridge Trail

Interpretive guide	Moderate	1.5 hours	4 km

After travelling through a boreal forest, hikers will arrive at a viewing platform. There are five interpretive stops explaining the relationship between the moose and the forest. Watch for moose near Raven Lake, and, if you are lucky, you may hear wolves howling. There are a few significant grades to climb.

Echo Pond Trail

Interpretive guide	Moderate	3–4 hours	6 km

Watch for moose and river otters. There are nine interpretive stops explaining the wildlife found in the boreal forest of this park

Hawk Ridge Trail

Backpacking	Strenuous	2–3 days	18 km

The trail travels to remote areas in the park through jack pine stands, grassy meadows and along granite cliffs. There are some significant grades to climb. Quotes from author and conservationist Grey Owl about the trail's surroundings enliven the trail map. Designated campsites have been established near secluded lakes.

KILLARNEY PROVINCIAL PARK
Killarney, Ontario P0M 2A0

Information: Call 705 287-2900
          Fax   705 287-2893

Operating season: May to March

Location: The park is on the north shore of Georgian Bay, northeast of Manitoulin Island. The main entrance is from Highway 637.

Natural features: The park is noted for its clear, turquoise lakes and the ivory-white La Cloche Mountains, a folded quartzite formation that covers three-quarters of the park. The trails follow white quartzite and pink granite ridges. As the park is in the transition zone between the northern boreal forest region and the Great Lakes–St. Lawrence Lowlands, there is a wide variety of plant and animal life. More than 100 species of bird breed here. Watch for Virginia rail, sandhill crane, American redstart and turkey vultures — all residents of this park.

All the trails are looped, 0.5 m wide, travelling over earth path and smooth rock surfaces. Conducted nature walks are offered.

Cranberry Bog Trail

Interpretive guide   Moderate   2.5 hours   4 km

The trail passes through several wetland areas. There are nine interpretive stops, featuring Wetland ecology. There are a few steep grades to climb.

Granite Ridge Trail

Interpretive guide   Moderate   1.5 hours   2 km

This earth path, meadow and rock surface trail features lookouts that provide views of the park's major landforms. There are 13 stops that explain different aspects of its cultural heritage and explore several vegetation habitats. There are a few steep grades to climb.

Chikanishing Trail

Interpretive displays Moderate   1.5 hours   3 km

This trail travels over outcrops of pink bedrock as well as through more level forested terrain. There are ten panels that explain the cultural history of the area, in particular the local history connected with Georgian Bay. Spectacular views are provided of Georgian Bay and area. There are a few steep grades to climb.

La Cloche Silhouette Trail

Backpacking   Very   7–10 days   100 km
Map   strenuous

This rugged trail circles the park travelling through forest and wetlands, over ridges and across valleys. Solitude, magnificent landscape, a variety of natural environments and crystal clear blue lakes make this backpacking trip unforgettable.

KILLBEAR PROVINCIAL PARK
Box 71, Nobel, Ontario P0G 1G0

Information: Call 705 342-5492
             Fax 705 342-1475

Operating season: May to October

Location: The park is north of Parry Sound, west of Highway 69 on Regional Road 559.

Natural features: The park's gently sloping sand beach is perhaps the finest on the eastern shore of Georgian Bay. Here, pine-clad rock outcrops plunge into the clear waters. Black spruce and cedar occupy the wet boggy areas, while species such as maple and beech grow on drier high ground.

Rare and endangered species of snake and turtle are found in the sedge meadow environment. Other protected habitats include a black spruce bog, a floating sphagnum bog and the park's remaining sand dunes.

All the trails are looped, 1.0 m wide, with an earth path or smooth rock surface. Conducted nature walks are offered.

Lookout Point Trail

Interpretive guide   Easy   1.5 hours   3.5 km

Walking through a forested area, the hiker will find nine interpretive stops with information on the life found within a hardwood forest: lichens, fungus and life after fire. Halfway, there is a magnificent view of Georgian Bay. There are some boardwalk sections and a few steep grades.

Twin Points Trail*

Interpretive guide   Easy   1 hour   2 km

Running first through a shady birch and maple forest, the trail crosses exposed smooth rock with mingled oak and pine trees. The eight interpretive stops explain the geological formation of the park. There are some boardwalk sections.

*Al's Picks, see page 90.

Lighthouse Point Trail

Hiking   Easy   1 hour   1.5 km

This trail takes you to the shores of Georgian Bay passing a navigation beacon at the halfway point.

MARTEN RIVER PROVINCIAL PARK
Marten River, Ontario P0H 1T0

Information: Call 705 892-2200
              Fax   705 892-2147

Operating dates: May to September

Location: The park is about 56 km north of North Bay in the direction of Temagami along Highway 11.

Natural features: The park has old-growth white pine left behind by loggers. The second-growth trees are maple, yellow birch, pines and black or white spruce. The diversity of forest plants in the transition between boreal forest and the Great Lakes–St. Lawrence Lowland forest has attracted a large number of birds.

Conducted nature walks are offered. Other trails include cycling, snowshoeing and snowmobiling using the park roads.

Transition/ Old-Growth White Pine Trail

Interpretive display   Moderate   2.5 hours   5 km

This looped, 2-m-wide trail runs over an earth path and boardwalk. There are 27 display panels that gives you details on the ecology of a bog, identification of tree and plant species and old-growth trees. The trail takes you through a stand of old-growth white pines, some over 300 years old. Connected to this trail is a second loop of 3 km used for short hikes and conducted nature walks.

MIKISEW PROVINCIAL PARK

Box 400, South River, Ontario P0A 1X0

Information: Call 705 386-7762
            Fax 705 386-2382

Operating season: June to September

Location: Off Highway 11, just west of South River between Huntsville and North Bay.

Natural features: Geologists have concluded that more than 10,000 years ago, Mikisew was an island surrounded by ancient Lake Algonquin.

Mikisew Trails

Hiking   Moderate   1.5 hours   1–3.2 km

This interconnected, looped trail system offers choices of three trail lengths. The trails are 1.5 m wide, travelling over earth path, meadow and boardwalk surfaces. There are several steep grades. You will walk through a mix of terrain, such as beaver meadows, and pine, birch, maple and cedar forests.

MISSISSAGI PROVINCIAL PARK

Box 81, Elliot Lake, Ontario P5A 2J6

Information: Call 705 848-2806
Fax 705 356-7471

Operating season: May to September

Location: The park is located above Lake Huron 25 km north of Elliott Lake and 190 km east of Sault Ste Marie. Access is via Highways 17 and 546 from the Sault, or Highways 108 and 639.

Natural features: Most of the park is undeveloped and provides solitude and a variety of easy or challenging trails. Fossils are found in the ancient rocks. Old logging and mining relics provide evidence throughout the park of long-ceased operations. There are massive old pines and a variety of other trees such as white birch and trembling aspen.

All the trails are looped, and run over an earth path. Interpretive trails are 1.5 m wide, while hiking trails are narrower. Other trails are available for cross-country skiing, snowshoeing and mountain biking.

Semiwite Creek Trail

Interpretive guide   Easy   1 hour   1.2 km

This trail is located near the Semiwite Creek. Side trails provide access to the creek. Numerous interpretive stops tell of the area's logging history and its unusual name.

Helenbar Lookout Trail

Interpretive guide   Moderate   2–4 hours   7 km

This trail's highlight is a viewing area 130 m high overlooking Helenbar Lake. A descriptive guide explains the glaciation and forest transition.

Flack Lake Nature Trail

Interpretive guide   Easy   45 minutes   0.8 km

The trail has 14 interpretive stops which explain aspects of the geology, forest and early logging practices within the park.

Cobre Lake Trail

| Hiking | Strenuous | 3–5 hours | 11 km |

A descriptive guide is available with information on the forest transition from Great Lakes–St. Lawrence Lowlands to boreal forest, as well as the logging and mining history of the area. The trail has many excellent viewing points.

McKenzie Trail

| Backpacking | Strenuous | 3–5 days | 22 km |
| Map | | | |

This trail takes you to remote sections of the park for camping beside its lakes. There are many steep grades and rocky areas to challenge hikers, with high cliffs and lookouts as rewards.

RESTOULE PROVINCIAL PARK
Restoule, Ontario P0H 2R0

Information: Call 705 729-2010
Fax 705 729-5428 (summer)
Fax 705 789-1610 (winter)

Operating season: April to November

Location: The park is at the end of Highway 534 on Restoule Lake, west of Highway 11.

Natural features: The park is secluded with towering bluffs of granite, and glassy lakes fringed with red pine. Plants such as wild cucumber and hobblebush are found here, and hemlock thrives in swampy areas — a favourite habitat for the commonly observed white-tailed deer. A variety of songbirds and shorebirds are found in the ponds and bogs of the low-lying wetlands.

There are three hiking trails. Plans are being made to make two of these trails interpretive. All the trails are looped, a minimum of 2 m wide, and travel mainly over earth paths. No guides or maps are available, but trails are clearly marked. Conducted nature walks are offered, and there is a cycling trail.

Tower Trail

Hiking	Moderate	3 hours	8 km

The fire tower, erected on top of a 100-m cliff, gives hikers a panoramic view of the surrounding forests. A brochure describing local historical events is provided. Hikers travel through a variety of forest types and geological features, and there are several steep slopes.

River Trail

Hiking	Easy	1.5 hours	3 km

The trail winds through a variety of forest tree types, with a wetland area that provides excellent birding opportunities.

Angels Point Trail

Hiking	Easy	2.5 hours	6 km

The route takes you through the forested areas of the park using an unpaved road. It is shared with cyclists.

SAMUEL DE CHAMPLAIN PROVINCIAL PARK

Box 147, Mattawa, Ontario P0H 1V0

Information: Call 705 744-2276
Fax 705 744-0587

Operating dates: May to October

Location: The park lies along the Mattawa River, 50 km east of North Bay, off Highway 17.

Natural features: The Mattawa River, a Canadian Heritage River, served as a major waterway for native peoples, explorers and the voyageurs. Although most of the original forest was logged before the 1880s, towering groves of mature hemlock and yellow birch still stand. A hybrid of wild rye and bottlebrush grass has been found nowhere else but in the park. Roses grow beside park roads and an array of cardinal flowers grows along the Horserace Rapids.

Wildlife includes moose, wolves, bear, and white-tailed deer, along with more than 200 species of bird including loons, common mergansers and wood ducks.

All the trails are looped, 1.5 m wide, travelling over an earth path with some boardwalk sections. There are conducted nature walks offered. The guide-books are in French and English. Use of the park roads for snowshoeing is allowed.

Kag Trail

Interpretive guide   Strenuous   1.5 hours   2.5 km

The trail travels through a stand of tall red pine to several lookouts. There are 12 interpretive stops, and each stop explores one aspect of the native peoples' beliefs in relation to the natural world. There are rocky surfaces and some very steep grades to climb.

Wabashkiki Trail*

Interpretive guide Moderate   1 hour   1 km

Travelling over an earth path, unpaved road and boardwalk, the trail features a floating boardwalk through a marsh. There are 12 interpretive stops. The guide describes, among other things, the interrelationships between land and water organisms.

* Al's Picks, see page 91.

Etienne Trail

Interpretive guide   Moderate to   1–6 hours   2.5–9 km
                      strenuous

There are four loops each with its own specific story. Excellent viewing points are provided overlooking the river and surrounding area.

The Ecology Loop is 2.5 km with three interpretive stops describing the essentials of a healthy natural environment. There are a few steep climbs along this loop.

The Geology Loop is a rugged 5-km trail with 12 interpretive stops explaining geological features, such as the Mattawa Valley, which is a major fault and outlet for the Great Lakes.

The Nature Loop is a rugged 8.5 km with 18 interpretive stops explaining the interrelationship between the rugged landscape and species that thrive here.

The History Loop is a rugged 9-km trail with 21 interpretive stops explaining the human history of this area, including that of the voyageurs and native peoples.

SIX MILE LAKE PROVINCIAL PARK
Box 340 , Coldwater, Ontario L0K 1E0

Information: Call 705 756-2746
Fax 705 756-4692 (May to Dec)
Fax 705 789-5948 (Dec to May)

Operating season: May to October

Location: The park is off Highway 400 (formerly Highway 69) at Exit 162, close to the southeastern shores of Georgian Bay.

Natural features: The park is part of the Great Lakes–St. Lawrence Lowlands forest region. The mixed forests here include oak, maple, poplar, and white pine trees. Hundreds of plants have been identified in the park including three species that are rare in Ontario: pond weed, yellow-eyed grass and smartweed.

Birdlife is abundant, both in the forests and the marshy areas. Ninety-one species have been identified, including the wood thrush, pileated woodpecker and turkey vulture. Rarer species sometimes seen are the yellow-throated vireo and Swainson's thrush.

Conducted nature hikes are offered.

Cambrian Trail

Hiking	Easy	1 hour	1.5 km

This linear trail is 0.5 m wide and runs over earth paths, smooth rock and board-walks. It takes you through a marshy area and oak forest to the top of a Canadian Shield outcrop. In the spring, pink lady's slipper and white trillium are abundant.

THE MASSASAUGA PROVINCIAL PARK

R.R. 2
Parry Sound, Ontario
P2A 2W8

Information: Call 705 378-2401
                Fax 705 378-0341

Operating season: May to October

Location: Note! These trails are accessible by water only. The park is on the shores of Georgian Bay, south of Parry Sound.

Natural features: This undisturbed section of the rocky Georgian Bay shoreline supports a large population of prairie warblers, rare in Ontario. Other rare species include the fox snake, Massasauga rattlesnake, hybrid toad and five-linked skink.

All the trails are looped with a minimum width of 2 m. Caution: The rocky shoreline and rugged inland terrain can be very slippery during wet weather.

The Baker Trail

Interpretive guide   Moderate   3 hours   5.5 km

Travelling over an earth path, beaver meadows and abandoned roadways, this trail has ten interpretive stops telling of early settlement in the area. Side trails take you to the shoreline, an ideal place for a picnic.

Wreck Island Trail

Interpretive guide   Moderate   1 hour   1.5 km

There are nine interpretive stops exploring fascinating examples of geological history. For those who find the trail too rugged, a shorter loop of about 800 m is provided.

Nipissing North Arm Orienteering Trail

Backpacking   Strenuous to   2–3 days   30 km
Map   very strenuous

This orienteering trail is aimed at hikers who welcome the challenge of walking on an unmarked route using a compass and map. There is no established trail.

The route covers a variety of terrain, and large areas of rock outcrops, cliffs and ridges are common. There are ten campsites and 12 destination interpretive posts that explain the diversity of the natural environment experienced along the trail. Caution: only hikers who are familiar with the use of maps and compass should attempt to use this trail.

WINDY LAKE PROVINCIAL PARK

199 Larch Street, Suite 404 Sudbury, Ontario P3E 5P9

Information: Call 705 966-2315 (after Mid-May)
              Fax 705 966-0565

Operating season: May to September

Location: The park is 40 km northwest of Sudbury on Highway 144.

Natural features: Millions of years ago, a meteorite crashed into the Earth in the region of what is now Sudbury creating a band of nickel called the Sudbury Nickel Irruptive. The park is situated at the point where this irruptive meets the Canadian Shield. Today there are seven operating nickel mines within a few kilometres of the park.

There are mountain-bike and cross-country ski trails available.

Lookout Tower Trail

Hiking   Moderate   1 hour   3 km

This looped, 1.5-m-wide earth path and boardwalk trail has two steep grades. It passes through a boreal forest and around a beaver pond and climbs up a jack pine ridge to a viewing platform offering a panoramic view of Windy Lake.

OTHER SPECIAL PLACES

French River Provincial Park

The trail through this park runs on earth and smooth rock. It is 1.5 km long and retraces the route of explorers, missionaries and voyageurs. There is no admission to the park, as it is non-operating. For more information call or write to Killarney Provincial Park.

Aubrey Falls Provincial Park

The 1-km interpretive trail through this park explains the fire history of the area and visits several waterfalls. For more information call or write to Mississagi Provincial Park.

AL'S PICKS

Arrowhead Provincial Park: Stubb's Falls Trail

This short hike is just right for those who enjoy a scenic walk after a picnic, or for car-weary travellers who want to stretch their legs and see a picturesque waterfall without taking up too much of their time.

Starting opposite the parking lot just before the bridge at Arrowhead Lake, you walk downstream along the shady banks of Little East River on a wide, clearly marked earth trail.

In spring, if you keep count as you walk along, you will be surprised at the number of wildflowers along this trail, including spring beauties, red and white trilliums, yellow trout lilies, squirrel corn and wild leeks.

During the summer the hardwood forest provides a cool and shady walk along the river. The most common tree found here is the sugar maple, familiar to everyone as the source of maple syrup, and as the leaf on the Canadian flag. The abundance of hardwoods makes it a spectacular fall colour hike.

Beside the falls, you'll see gigantic boulders sitting amongst the hardwood trees. These are known as glacial erratics, and they were carried and deposited here by glaciers.

Upon reaching the waterfalls the view from the wooden and steel bridge shows water cascading down over several 2-m-high rock chutes composed of granite and gneiss. If you want to get a closer view of the waterfalls, follow the river embankment to the right before the bridge. Carefully descend a natural rock stairway to a smooth rocky shelf at the water's edge. This is a pleasant place to relax and listen to the soothing sounds of the falls.

After crossing the bridge, you climb a steep steel stairway. On this side of the river you experience a different type of forest. Here, white pine, balsam fir and white birch grow at varying heights, above wildflowers such as bunchberry, Canada mayflower and goldthread. The trail ends on the main road where you will turn left, descend a short hill, and cross the main bridge to the parking lot where you began.

Killbear Provincial Park: Twins Point Trail

For most of us, a few deeply etched images characterize Ontario's wild landscape: the spire-like silhouettes of black spruce; steep rock cliffs plunging into Lake Superior's cold, deep waters; the white quartzite knolls and crystalline lakes of the La Cloche Mountains and, perhaps most familiar of all, the pink granite and gneiss outcrops and wind-swept pines of Georgian Bay's Thirty Thousand Islands. This trail gives you the opportunity to explore this world of rock, water and pine. As well, an excellent trail guide is available to explain how ice and water has sculpted the landscape over the ages.

Twin Points Trail begins at the park's day-use parking lot, where it is readily accessible to both day users and campers. While the first portion of the trail is level and covered with a soft layer of woodchips, the going gets a bit rougher as the trail narrows and gives way to rocky and earthen surfaces. Of course, a trail that explores rock outcrops is necessarily somewhat rugged and there a few short, steep climbs. Nevertheless, healthy adults and robust children should have no trouble travelling this trail in less than an hour. Sturdy footwear is recommended.

The trail begins in a shady sugar maple and white birch forest, but then moves into a mixed community of oaks and pines growing among smooth rock outcrops. The interpretive trail guide explains in non-technical terms how glaciers helped form this rugged scene. It is a fascinating story that began 1.8 billion years ago with the upheaval of towering mountains and that continues today with waves lapping on the sandy Kilcoursie Bay beach. Eight marked stops along the trail refer to numbered entries in the trail guide. For example, stop 4 explains how debris-laden water flowing under the glacier formed the smooth surfaces of the rocky outcrops all around you.

After meandering across a series of rocky outcrops the well-marked trail reaches the Georgian Bay shoreline. There are excellent views of a number of rocky headlands and islands caressed by the Bay's clear, clean waters. Offshore, cormorants and loons may be seen diving for fish. You may be tempted to wade in the cool waters, but a little caution is needed because the wet rocks are slippery.

After reaching Georgian Bay, the trail skirts along the shore, passing a pristine sand beach situated in a snug cove. This is a great spot to sit and simply watch the waves lap the shore, as they have for millions of years. Photographers will enjoy the beach and the surrounding rock outcrops, particularly the pink rocks, covered with lichen and algae of various hues, and topped with wind-swept white pines. From the beach the trail returns to the parking lot about 50 m from the entry point.

Here is an easy, almost-level trail that has a little of everything for each member of the family: wildlife viewing, marsh, water, rock and a beautiful forest, all in a walk that takes less than an hour. Expect to see a variety of birdlife because of the diversity of habitat. The trail name, *wabashkiki*, means "marsh" in Ojibwa, and this is our destination.

Following an abandoned roadway for a short distance between speckled alder trees, the trail quickly narrows and we enter a swampy, mixed forest, with tall silver maple and black ash trees shading high bush cranberry shrubs, Virgina creeper vines and ostrich fern.

Just ahead the orange spotted touch-me-not can be found blooming in mid-summer. This tall succulent annual with pendulous flowers is popular with hummingbirds. If you touch the ripe seed pod a coiled spring inside bursts the pod, dispersing the seeds, giving rise to its name.

As you are walking along the shoreline of the Amable du Fond River, watch for muskrats, beaver, water shrews and fish. The most common sighting will be the green frog. A floating boardwalk, approximately 70 m long, is just ahead. You have now reached the marsh, with all its life. The frogs are plentiful here. Tread carefully! For more of nature's beauty, there are flowering plants such as the white water lily, white arrowhead and purple pickerel weed. The boardwalk travels over the marsh and takes you to an island called the "Quiet Zone." Take a moment to stop and listen to the natural world. The island has a massive white pine tree. Further along the trail you may notice something strange, eastern white cedar trees that have no leaves or branches below 2 m. During the winter the deer gather here to eat these leaves resulting in a uniform lower foliage height called a browse line.

You are now travelling alongside Moore Lake. Stop and rest at the large bedrock outcrop and take in the tranquility of the lake. In July, this is a good place to pick some blueberries. Artificial nesting boxes have been placed along the return portion of the trail. These duck nesting boxes have been home to wood ducks, goldeneyes and hooded mergansers. You might see them on the Lake. By now, the end of the trail is in sight.

ALGONQUIN/CENTRAL REGION

PARKS OF THE REGION

Algonquin	Darlington	McRae Point
Balsam Lake	Emily	Petroglyphs
Bass Lake	Mark S. Burnham	Sibbald Point

ALGONQUIN PROVINCIAL PARK
Box 219, Whitney , Ontario K0J 2M0

Information: Call 705 633-5572
                       613 622-2828 (Visitor Centre)
              Fax 613 637-2864
              Web site www.algonquinpark.on.ca

Operating season: Open all year

Location: The park is a three hours' drive north from Toronto. The most popular area of the park, the Highway 60 corridor, is accessible via Huntsville to the west or Pembroke to the east. Other access points are on Highway 17 to the east or north, or Highway 11 to the west.

Natural features: The park is full of wild and beautiful lakes and forests, bogs and rivers, cliffs and beaches. Established in 1893, Algonquin was Ontario's first provincial park. The area is a transition zone between the broad-leaved, deciduous forests of the south and the coniferous forests of the north.

The essence of the park is held in its vast interior maple hills, rocky ridges, spruce bogs, and thousands of lakes, ponds and streams. The fall colours are superb.

The meeting of south and north has resulted in more than 250 bird species being recorded in the park. Many southern and overseas birders make special trips to Algonquin just to see northern specialties such as the grey jay and spruce grouse, not to mention the rich variety of warblers or the common loon, found nesting on just about every lake. Unforgettable experiences are seeing moose and hearing howling wolves.

A total of 16 interpretive trails and three long-distance hiking trails run throughout the park. Most visitors enter on Highway 60, which traverses the southwestern corner. From the West Gate (Km 0) to the East Gate (Km 56) there are kilometre markers fastened to most information posts along the highway to help visitors to locate the 13 interpretive trails and two of the three backpacking trails. For example the Whiskey Rapids Trail is located at Km 7.2. There are two interpretive trails and a backpacking trail located on the east side of the park. There is one interpretive trail located at Brent on the north side. Conducted nature walks and school tours are available. All trails are looped and well-marked, and a minimum of 0.5 m to 1.0 m wide. Unless noted the travel surfaces are mostly earth path. Other trails available are cycling, mountain biking, horseback riding, cross-country skiing, dogsledding and snowshoeing.

An interpretive stop is enriched by using the trail guide.

Whiskey Rapids Trail (Km 7.2)

| Interpretive guide | Moderate | 1.5 hours | 2.1 km |

The trail travels along the scenic Oxtongue River through black spruce and balsam fir stands and culminates in a close view of the rapids. The 11 interpretive stops along the trail explore the ecology of the river.

Hardwood Lookout Trail (Km 13.8)

| Interpretive guide | Moderate | 1 hour | 0.8 km |

The trail has ten interpretive stops that discuss the ecology of a deciduous (hardwood) forest. A scenic lookout with the bonus of a side trail to a rare stand of red spruce is offered. There are some steep climbs.

Mizzy Lake Trail (Km 15.4)

| Interpretive guide | Moderate | 4–6 hours | 11 km |

This trail has a 2-km optional spur. The trail travels over earth path and boardwalk and there are 12 interpretive stops along the trail highlighting the wildlife of the area. A total of nine small lakes and ponds are visited, increasing your chances of seeing wildlife such as moose and beaver.

Peck Lake Trail (Km 19.2)

| Interpretive guide | Moderate | 1 hour | 1.9 km |

The trail meanders around the Peck Lake periphery though a coniferous forest. The surface is mostly earth path with a small section of boardwalk. The trail has 11 stops each discussing a certain aspect of the ecology of the lake.

Track and Tower Trail (Km 25)

| Interpretive guide | Moderate | 2 hours | 7.7 km |

There is a main loop and an optional side trail (5.5 km one way) leading east towards Mew Lake campground. The main loop takes you to an old fire tower, past several old railway trestles, to a scenic lookout. The main loop has 11 stops explaining the history of the area. If you decide to take the side trail, two additional interpretive stops are provided.

Hemlock Bluff Trail (Km 27.2)

Interpretive guide   Moderate   2 hours   3.5 km

The main features of this trail are the fine stands of hemlock and an excellent view of Jack Lake. There are nine stops explaining key research findings in the park.

Bat Lake Trail (Km 30)

Interpretive guide   Moderate   2.5 hours   5.6 km

The trail travels through a variety of forest types, including a mature hemlock stand, and passes a lookout, a bog and an acidic lake. There are 12 interpretive stops that examine basic ecology.

Two Rivers Trail (Km 31.0)

Interpretive guide   Moderate   1 hour   2.1 km

The trail travels through a young forest and leads to a cliff top overlooking the North Madawaska River. There are nine stops explaining the importance of change in the natural forest.

Centennial Ridges Trail (Km 37.6)

Interpretive guide   Strenuous   3–4 hours   10 km

This trail offers spectacular views along two high ridges. The guide has 11 stops that discuss the contributions made to the Park by selected people over the course of its first century.

Lookout Trail (Km 39.7)

Interpretive guide   Moderate   1 hour   1.9 km

The trail climbs up through a young forest to the top of a high cliff, then follows the cliff brow for 100 m. The view, especially in the fall, is breathtaking as it sweeps over a panorama of outstanding scenery. The trail guide has eight stops that explain geological features such as an erratic, seen along the trail.

Booth's Rock Trail (Km 40.3)

Interpretive guide   Moderate   2 hours   5.1 km

This trail climbs to the cliff known as Booth's Rock and descends by wooden stairway to the far side of the lookout. A magnificent view of Rock and Whitefish lakes and hundreds of square kilometres of the park can be seen. After visiting the ruins of the Barclay Estate, walkers return on an old railway bed to the start of the trail. The guide has 11 stops that explain the impact of humans on the environment.

Spruce Bog Boardwalk (Km 42.5)*

Interpretive guide Easy   1 hour   1.5 km

The trail is half boardwalk and half earth path, and 1.0 m wide. It crosses two separate bogs, the Sunday Creek Bog and a small kettle bog. There are 11 interpretive stops along the way. The boardwalk enables you to see at close range the ecology of a northern black spruce bog. Some of the flora you will see and smell are lush green carpets of moss, sedges, leatherleaf, sweet gale, speckled alder, Labrador tea and pitcher plants. This trail provides the Highway 60 corridor's most accessible birdwatching for boreal species such as spruce grouse and yellow-bellied flycatcher.

*Al's Picks, see page 108.

Beaver Pond Trail (Km 45.2)

Interpretive guide   Moderate   1 hour   2 km

The trail winds through low bush and around two beaver ponds and allows you to explore the role of the beaver in this natural environment. There are nine stops along the trail that explain its presence, activities and influence.

The Western Uplands Backpacking Trail (Km 3)

Backpacking   Strenuous   2–6 days   32–88 km
Map

Depending on how many loops of the trail you choose to do, round trips can take from two days to a week. The trails are through deciduous (hardwood) uplands. A detailed map, regulations and information are available from the park information building or Friends of Algonquin Park.

Highland Backpacking Trail (Km 29.7)

Backpacking   Strenuous   2–3 days   19–35 km
Map

There are two loops (19 km and 35 km) suitable for trips of two or more days. The short trail circles Provoking Lake while the longer trail travels to Head and Harness Lakes. A detailed map, regulations and information are available from the park information centre or Friends of Algonquin Park.

Logging Museum Trail (Km 54)

Interpretive guide   Easy   45 minutes   1 km

There are 20 exhibits along this two-metre-wide, gravel trail. It loops past a reconstructed caboose logging camp and exhibits depicting logging techniques over a 150-year span.

EASTERN SECTION OF ALGONQUIN PARK

Access is from Highway 17 just west of Pembroke at the first Petawawa exit. Turn south on Renfrew County Road 26 (opposite the airport sign). After travelling only 0.3 km, turn right on Achray Road South. This road is paved for the next 9 km. Starting from the point where the pavement ends, every kilometre is marked with a black and white sign. These markings continue to the end of public access at Lake Travers (72 kms). The two interpretive trails will be referred to using kilometre signs as done for the Highway 60 trails.

Barron Canyon Trail (Km 28.9)

Interpretive guide   Moderate   1 hour   1.5 km

This trail leads to and runs along the north rim of the spectacular, 100-m-deep Barron canyon. The guide uses six stops to explain the formation and history of the canyon. Caution: This trail travels by an unfenced cliff, keep children and pets under close control at all times.

Berm Lake Trail (Km 37.8)

Interpretive guide   Moderate   2 hours   4.5 km

The trail circles Berm Lake and runs through pine and oak forests typical of the area. The guide has ten stops that discuss the ecology of a pine forest.

Eastern Pines Backpacking Trail

Backpacking	Strenuous	1–2 days	6–14.8 km
Map		or more	

The shorter of the trail's two loops may be easily walked in one day, but camping on it is permitted as well as on the second, longer loop. The return leg of the trail is shared with the Berm Lake Interpretive trail. A detailed map, regulations and information are available from the park information centre or Friends of Algonquin Park.

NORTHERN SECTION OF THE PARK

Situated on Cedar Lake along the Petawawa River, Brent is located 32 km south from Deux-Rivieres on Highway 17. The road is extremely rough.

Brent Crater Trail

Interpretive guide	Strenuous	1.5 hours	2 km

The crater was formed when a meteorite crashed here about 450 million years ago. From a wooden observation tower overlooking the crater the trail descends to its floor before looping back to the starting point. There are six stops that relate some of the geological and historical significance of this unique feature.

BALSAM LAKE PROVINCIAL PARK
R.R. 1, Kirkfield, Ontario K0M 2B0

Information: Call 705 454-1077
             Fax 705 454-2610

Operating season: May to October

Location: On Victoria County Road 48 between Kirkfield and Coboconk, 6 km west of Highway 35.

Natural features: The park is located along a chain of lakes that are linked, via river and canal, to the Trent-Severn Waterway. The rolling, reforested woodlands are home to a variety of wildlife including porcupine, beaver and white-tailed deer.

These clearly marked trails are both looped and approximately 1.0 m wide, travelling over earth path, wood chips and boardwalk. Conducted nature walks are offered.

Lookout Nature Trail*

Interpretive guide   Easy   1.5 hours   3 km

The trail has 11 interpretive stops explaining both the geology and forest habitats of the area. Starting on an esker, the trail passes through a variety of habitats such as a cedar swamp, deciduous forest and open meadows, finally reaching a lookout tower. There are a couple of steep grades. The view from the tower provides a vista of meadows, rolling hills, moraines and kames.

*Al's Picks, see page 110.

Plantation Trail

Interpretive guide   Easy   1.5 hours   2 km

Along the trail the nine interpretive stops explain, among other things, forest management and glaciation. There is an option at the halfway point: return to the start of the trail or continue on a second loop for an additional 2 km. The trail travels through mostly open grasslands and a 20-year-old pine plantation. In the open areas you will find wildflowers, and wild raspberries and strawberries.

BASS LAKE PROVINCIAL PARK
Box 2178, Orillia, Ontario L3V 6S1

Information: Call 705 326-7054
             Fax 705 329-6028

Operating season: May to September

Location: The park is located 5 km west of Orillia, off Highway 12.

Natural features: The park's beach is the remains of a former bay along the shoreline of ancient Lake Algonquin. Its open fields, forest and wetland area provides a diversity of habitat for all types of wildlife such as deer, and about 124 other bird species including loons and herons.

The trail is barrier-free for approximately 0.5 km. There is no trail map or guide except the park's information sheet (tabloid), but the trail is clearly marked. The park is linked to the long-distance Ganaraska Hiking Trail.

Waterview Trail

| Hiking | Easy | 1 hour | 2.5 km |

This looped trail starts in the day-use area where it is paved for 0.5 km. It is a minimum of 1.5 m in width, providing easy and barrier-free access. It passes within close viewing distance of Bass Lake. This portion of the trail includes easy access to washrooms and picnicking facilities. The remaining trail consists of a short boardwalk over a wetland area, followed by a surface of granular limestone screenings. The trail follows the water's edge for another 1.5 km, then loops back to the picnic grounds. It provides an excellent overview of the wildlife, geography and history of Bass Lake. An interpretive trail guide is being produced.

DARLINGTON PROVINCIAL PARK

R.R. 2, Bowmanville, Ontario L1C 3K3

Information: Call 905 436-2036
             Fax 905 436-3729
         Web site www.cwise.com/darlpark.htm

Operating season: All year

Location: The park is located east of Toronto, past Oshawa along Highway 401. Turn south at Courtice Road (Exit 425). Follow park signs to Darlington Park Road.

Natural features: The park is located on the shores of Lake Ontario. Numerous bird species and waterfowl use the shoreline and marsh areas in the park as resting and feeding areas during migration. Along the Burk Trail there is a scenic lookout that provides a panoramic view of McLaughlin Bay and Lake Ontario. Located just west of the park is the famous birding sanctuary called Second Marsh, which is the largest remaining coastal wetland on the north shore of Lake Ontario.

All trails are clearly marked. The trails are between 0.5 m and 1.5 m wide on earth paths. Conducted nature walks are offered.

Robinson Creek Trail

Interpretive guide   Easy   1 hour   1 km

This looped trail starts and ends at the Visitor Information Centre. There are 15 interpretive stops along Robinson Creek. A unique natural trivia guide examines the variety of vegetation found along the creek. There are two wooden bridges that cross Robinson Creek.

Burk Trail

Hiking   Moderate   1 hour   1 km

This looped trail travels through open fields, meadows and mature forest with some steep inclines. A pioneer cemetery and scenic lookout are features along the trail. The trail connects with the McLaughlin Trail.

Waterfront Trail

Hiking   Easy   45 minutes   2.6 km

The full Waterfront Trail is a 350-km long-distance, multi-use linear hiking trail along the shore of Lake Ontario from Niagara-on-the-Lake to Trenton. A portion of the trail is located within the park. A guidebook is available: see Recommended Reading at page 168. A "walking only" section branches off for closer access to Lake Ontario and reconnects to the main trail within the park.

McLaughlin Bay Trail

Hiking   Easy   1 hour   1.5 km (return)

This linear trail follows the edge of McLaughlin Bay, and in partnership with the Friends of Second Marsh, provides a link to Second Marsh and public access to the marsh ecosystem. There are many birdwatching opportunities.

EMILY PROVINCIAL PARK

R.R. 4, Omemee, Ontario K0L 2W0

Operating season: May to October

Information: Call 705 799-5170
             Fax 705 799-2433

Location: The park is on the Pigeon River between Lindsay and Peterborough on County Road 10, north off Highway 7.

Natural features: The Pigeon River, part of the Kawartha Lakes system, winds through the park. The shoreline marshes and wet cedar woods provide a specialized habitat for birds and plant life.

Conducted nature walks are offered.

Marsh Boardwalk Trail

Hiking	Easy	1 hour	0.8 km

This loop is 1.5 m wide, travelling over earth path, wood chip and boardwalk. There is access to a cattail marsh and a sphagnum island with a viewing platform. An active osprey nest can be observed from this point.

MARK S. BURNHAM PROVINCIAL PARK

R.R. 4, Omemee, Ontario K0L 2W0

Operating season: May to October

Information: Call 705 799-5170
             Fax 705 799-2433

Location: The park is on Highway 7 just east of Peterborough.

Natural features: Lofty stands of old growth beech, maple, elm and hemlock over 30 m tall are found in the park. It is situated on a drumlin, a smoothly contoured, oval-shaped hill of boulders and other sediment deposited by glaciers as they retreated.

Mark S. Burnham Trail

| Hiking | Easy | 1 hour | 2.5 km |

This double loop is 1.5 m in width, with a travel surface of earth path and wood chips. It winds through an old-growth woodlot. The first loop takes 45 minutes to walk, and the second, 15 minutes. In the spring there is an extravagant display of wildflowers.

MCRAE POINT PROVINCIAL PARK

Box 2178, Orillia, Ontario L3V 6S1

Information: Call 705 325-7290
705 326-7054 (off season)
Fax 705 329-6028

Operating season: May to October

Location: Access is via Highway 12, about 18 km from Orillia on the northeast shore of Lake Simcoe.

Natural features: Almost 500 species of vascular plants grow in the park, including maidenhair and rattlesnake ferns. Seventy-nine species of bird inhabit the area, including the yellow-throated vireo and pileated woodpecker.

There is a descriptive trail pamphlet explaining the natural features of the area.

Pathless Woods Trail

| Hiking | Easy | 1 hour | 1.2 km |

This linear trail is 1.0 m wide and travels on boardwalk for half the distance and earth path for the rest. It ends at a campground road. The trail meanders through a cedar and mixed forest area, and crosses a cedar swamp. This area is thick with ferns growing near the trail. There is a lookout point with a good view of Lake Simcoe. The last half of the trail follows the shoreline leading back to the trailhead.

PETROGLYPHS PROVINCIAL PARK

General Delivery, Woodview, Ontario K0L 3E0

Information: Call 705 877-2552 (Mid-May to Thanksgiving)
              705 332-3940 (off season)
        Fax 613 332-0608

Operating season: May to October

Location: The park is located 55 km northeast of Peterborough off Highway 28.

Natural and cultural features: The park contains large stands of red and white pine, sugar maple and red oak. There are some active wetland areas in the park, created by beavers. In all seasons, much of the park is carpeted with a profusion of wildflowers. Deer are often seen, and birds include grey jays, American goldfinches and ruffed grouse. A rare and fascinating collection of petroglyphs (rock carvings) give the park its name. All visitors are welcome at the protective structure where they are preserved. The glyphs depict such things as turtles, snakes, humans and other beings and objects. Altogether, they number about 900. This is one of the largest concentrations of aboriginal rock art in North America. Members of a contemporary native band, the Ojibwa Anishinabe, call the site Kinomagewapkong, "The Rocks that Teach."

Special attention is required to follow the trail markers as most of the trails do connect with each other at certain points. The trails are half a metre wide and travel over earth path and smooth rock surfaces with some boardwalk sections. Conducted nature walks are offered. A hiking trail map is available.

Caution: If you want to hike the High Falls Trail it is recommended you start before noon as the park closes and gates are locked at 5:30 pm.

Nanabush Trail*

Interpretive guide   Easy   1.5 hours   5.5 km

This looped trail traverses a wide range of terrain from bridged wetlands to the Precambrian Shield rock outcrops. Minnow Lake is a picturesque northern lake surrounded by high granite stone. Using the trail guide, hikers will visit 11 rock cairns connecting native legends with points of interest near the trail.

*Al's Picks, see page 111.

Marsh Trail

| Hiking | Moderate | 2.5 hours | 7 km |

The trail leads you through a dense pine forest and low wetlands to a higher Precambrian Shield environment. At one point it joins all the other trails, allowing you to return to the start of the trail. There are steep grades to climb.

West Day Use Trail

| Hiking | Moderate | 1.5 hours | 5 km |

This looped trail takes you through a wide range of environments, from low wetlands and marshes, with poplar and cedar tree stands, to the higher Precambrian Shield of oak, birch, spruce, and pine trees. There are some short, steep grades.

High Falls Trail

| Hiking | Moderate | 3 hours | 16 km (return) |

This linear trail has short steep grades in certain sections. It crosses bridged wetlands and higher rock outcrops, and gives visitors an opportunity to see the wide range of the Canadian Shield landscape. It ends at a series of tall rapids — an ideal spot for a picnic.

SIBBALD POINT PROVINCIAL PARK
R.R. 2, Sutton West, Ontario L0E 1R0

Information: Call 905 722-8061
Fax 905 722-5416

Operating season: May to October

Location: It is located on the south shore of Lake Simcoe, near Highway 48.

Natural features: The park is forested, with marshes and sandy beaches.

Both trails are looped and 1.5 m in width travelling over earth path and gravel surfaces. There are plans to make one of the trails an interpretive trail, but at present only one trail is clearly marked. Conducted nature walks are offered.

Cedar Trail

Hiking   Easy   1 hour   2.5 km

The route takes you through a deciduous and coniferous forest that was once farmland.

Hardwood Trail

Hiking   Easy   45 minutes   2.1 km

The trail takes you through a deciduous (hardwood) forest, with tree species such as beech, maple and white birch. Near the end of the trail there is a pleasant view of a small wetland area.

OTHER SPECIAL PLACES

Peter's Woods Provincial Nature Reserve

The most significant feature of the reserve is the old-growth forest of sugar maple, American beech and white pine. Contact the Ministry of Natural Resources, Ontario Parks for more information.

Indian Point Provincial Park

There are over 100 species of trees, shrubs and spring flowers and about 100 species of resident bird. Contact Balsam Lake Provincial Park for more information.

AL'S PICKS

Algonquin Provincial Park: Spruce Bog Boardwalk

This is a short and easy walk through a different side of Algonquin. It circles around the Sunday Creek bog and a small kettle bog. It is ideal for children because half the trail is built on boardwalk enabling everyone to see at close range the little-known world of a spruce bog. Using the excellent trail guide at the start of the trail, you will stop at numbered posts and read about some of the history and ecology of the bog. You will learn that in all its stages the bog water is distinctly acidic, contains almost no oxygen and has very few dissolved salts and minerals. As every gardener knows, vital nutrients such as calcium, nitrogen and phosphorus are required by all plants, as well as humans and other animals, to live and grow.

The trail starts and ends on an earth path heavily impacted by use (a testimony to how popular this trail is with visitors). After walking through a forest

of black spruce, poplar, maple and white birch, you'll arrive at the start of the boardwalk stretching over the Sunday Creek bog.

One of the first plants to be seen and the most important in the bog is called *Carex lasiocarpa*. Without it the bog would simply not be here. It is a sedge plant, and what is unique about this plant is that its rootstocks do not have to be buried in mud but can and do grow out into water. The network of sedge roots forms the floating mat in which other plants take root.

Further down the boardwalk if you look on your left just past interpretive stop 4, you will see the vegetation is rather different closer to the creek. Here, shrubs such as sweet gale and speckled alder have been able to get established because the creek water is less acidic and carries nutrients.

At the same stop to your right, looking at the expanse of open bog, there are two kinds of plants. The densely growing shrub called leatherleaf, and the carpet of green sphagnum moss growing beneath it.

As we leave the bog the nature of the flora changes to dryer land varieties. Black spruce trees and Labrador tea shrubs can be seen, but because of the acidic nature of the bog the black spruce grows in a nutrient-starved base of organic matter. As a result it grows very slowly — even the 30-year-old trees near the boardwalk are very small.

The bogs are full of wildlife and the most visible are the birds. This trail is one of the most famous places in Ontario to see spruce grouse, a northern species rarely found south of Algonquin. In April and May, displays and "flutter-flights" of courting males can be seen. In summer, the early morning or late afternoon are times of increased feeding activity for the grouse. While you might encounter the birds along any part of the trail, there are at least two sections where more frequent observations have been made. They are between interpretive stops 1 and 2 and near the start of the trail. The golden-crowned kinglet is the tiny insect hunter whose high-pitched lisping call mingles with the sound of swaying spruce tops during June and July. The spruce forests are famous for the grey jay, formerly called Canada jay or sometimes whiskey Jack, and during a summer evening it is a good place to hoot for owls. The range of insect varieties is too long to list and depends on the time of year. Water striders, beetles, no-see-ums, moths and others are common insects.

After curving around the kettle bog the trail emerges from the black spruce woods and crosses a bridge. This is your last close-up view of the bog before exiting the trail over an abandoned roadway that takes you back to the start.

For a fine overview of the bog, you may want to climb to the top of the rock cut near interpretive stop 10. From here you can see the main features of the Sunday Creek bog: the meandering creek, the two broad mats covered with leatherleaf, and the army of black spruce on the far side. Finally, this trail is a good winter snowshoeing trail.

Balsam Lake Provincial Park: Lookout Nature Trail

The Lookout Nature Trail concentrates on the park's geological and natural features. While not long, it gives the hiker an opportunity to climb a tower for a spectacular view of the park and surrounding area.

The first section of the trail gives you a chance to examine the effects of the most recent of the park's major geological events. As the glaciers of ten to twelve thousand years ago began to melt, channels of water pushed through the ice pack, gradually tunnelling beneath it. These channels or rivers picked up and moved sand, gravel and boulders. As the melting slowed, the under-ice rivers deposited their burdens, leaving behind long, sinuous ridges of stones surrounded by finer and finer sand. The ridges are called eskers and you are walking on top of one.

There are many eskers in Ontario and they vary in length from this small one shorter than 2 km — to one of Ontario's longest, at 249 km. The width of eskers varies from less than a metre to over 30 m. This park's esker is less than 5 m wide.

After about ten minutes the trail leaves the esker and swings to the right passing through a small woodland opening where in spring wildflowers grow in abundance. At the edge of this clearing, you arrive at a recently reconstructed footbridge traversing a cedar swamp flooded by beavers. From the bridge the water is dark and murky but it's an excellent place to see a variety of birds such as mallard and black ducks.

Lookout tower, Balsalm Lake Provincial Park.

The trail continues through a large stand of eastern white cedar, making an enjoyably cool summer walk with the refreshing scent of cedar. The trail exits into an open area dominated by sumacs and tall grasses. Just ahead is the viewing tower built on top of a kame. A kame is a low round hill created by glaciers. This lookout tower is located on the tallest of many kames in the area, allowing for good views over Balsam Lake, and the surrounding cottages and farmland. From the tower there is an excellent chance you will see turkey vultures or red-tailed hawks soaring over the abandoned farm fields in the distance.

Leaving the tower, the trail leads back down through a large open field before re-entering a small cool gully filled with ash, maple and cedar trees. This open area in early morning or late evening provides a good opportunity to see white-tailed deer. Further along the trail the canopy begins to close in giving you a sense of wilderness solitude. The trail travels over a few short boardwalk sections and reconnects with the main esker path leading back to the start of the trail.

Petroglyphs Provincial Park: Nanabush Trail

Amid the stands of red and white pine, interspersed with pockets of spruce and mixed hardwoods such as white birch, sugar maple and red oak is a flat marble rock, part of the Canadian Shield, where Algonkian-speaking Ojibwa left carvings — petroglyphs — of shamans, other humans, snakes, turtles, thunderbirds and arrows. They tell a story that spans over a thousand years. Before hiking the Nanabush Trail, a visit to this sacred site is highly recommended.

The Nanabush Trail is a short, narrow and relatively easy walk through a mixed forest with exposed marble outcroppings interspersed with low wetland areas. There are two boardwalks and a bridge that will take you across the marshes and swamps. The main part of the trail provides access for two other trails, and after a short distance, coloured trail markers make each trail easy to follow. The red markers indicate the Nanabush Trail as it loops around the north shore of Minnow Lake. There is a steep hill at one end.

The name Nanabush, or "Teacher" is from an Ojibwa story about the Great Spirit, Kitchi Manitou, who sent a teacher, Nanabush, to help the people survive the harsh climate by showing them uses of various animals and plants. As you travel along this trail, Nanabush will introduce you to the mythological and natural world of the Ojibwa. Using the trail guide you will read the story of how the white birch got its black marks, the chipmunk got its stripes, and where white lilies came from.

The stories are told using 11 interpretive stops made of stone piles (cairns) as markers for points of interest. The cairns describe the natural and cultural features of the trail, using symbols to represent beliefs held by the Ojibwa.

The trail is surrounded by the Peterborough Crown Game Preserve, so there are many white-tailed deer in the area. The chance of seeing deer is greater if you make very little noise! Like the first inhabitants please respect the natural surroundings. The last cairn is the "Prayer to a deer slain by a hunter." A short distance ahead you will turn left to return to the start of the trail.

SOUTHEASTERN REGION

PARKS OF THE REGION

Bon Echo
Bonnechere
Charleston Lake
Ferris
Fitzroy

Frontenac
Lake St. Peter
Murphys Point
Presqu'ile
Sandbanks

Sharbot Lake
Silent Lake
Silver Lake
Voyageur

BON ECHO PROVINCIAL PARK

R.R. 1, Cloyne, Ontario K0H 1K0

Information: Call 613 336-2228

Operating season: May to October

Location: The park is halfway between Belleville and Renfrew on Highway 41, about 10 km north of the village of Cloyne.

Natural features: A spectacular 1.5-km-long sheer cliff rises 100 m above the deep, dark waters of Mazinaw Lake. The rock is a special place for many reasons, but its most intriguing feature is the scores of ancient pictographs painted just above the waterline. These evocative images represent one of the largest such concentrations in North America.

Park flora and fauna are a blend of northern and southern species: trees such as spruce and pine mix with maple and beech; timber wolves and moose co-exist with prairie warblers and five-linked skinks, and the park nurtures such unusual plants as lance-leaved violets and yellow-eyed grass.

All the trails are a minimum of 0.5 m wide, travelling mostly over earth or rocky surfaces. Five of the trails are looped. Conducted nature walks are offered.

Cliff Top Trail

Interpretive guide   Moderate   1 hour   1.5 km (return)

This linear trail, 1.0 m wide, and with an earth and rock surface, provides a well-engineered stairway for the steep climb to the top of the Bon Echo Rock. Access to the trail is by ferry. There are three viewing lookouts, and one, 100 m high, overlooks the lake. Fall colours make this a favourite trail, and there are 13 interpretive stops, each explaining the basics of the geology and ecology of this area.

High Pines Trail

Interpretive guide   Moderate   1 hour   1.4 km

The trail passes through a forest of deciduous and coniferous trees. There are 12 interpretive stops describing the ecology of the forest. There are views of Lake Mazinaw and Bon Echo rock.

Shield Trail*

Interpretive guide Moderate   2 hours   4.8 km

The trail travels through an area now forested but once settled by early pioneers. There are 14 interpretive stops that explain the early settlement and interaction of people with the Canadian Shield environment. Hikers will walk by a beaver pond in the process of becoming a beaver meadow.

*Al's Picks, see page 134.

Kishkebus Canoe Trail

Interpretive guide   Strenuous   5–6 hours   2.1 km

This unique water trail, a short canoe route, includes four portages. There are nine interpretive stops, explaining special features of the park, including the pictographs, specially adapted trees, and the Old Walt memorial. You will have to leave your canoe to see some of them.

Abes and Essens Trail

Hiking   Strenuous   2–7 hours   4–17 km
Backpacking

This trail has three loops, with some boardwalk sections, and it travels around two lakes. It can be either hiked in a day or backpacked — campsites are available. Hikers will see gigantic boulders, evidence of old logging methods, panoramic views, a kettle lake and forests of pine, poplar, maple and white birch.

Bon Echo Creek Trail

Hiking   Easy   45 minutes   2 km (return)

This linear trail explores the creek bank habitat. It provides plenty of opportunities for bird watching.

Pet Exercise Trail

Hiking   Moderate   1 hour   2.4 km

This trail provides access to a unique area where many southern plants such as cardinal flowers grow. This is the only area in the park where pets are allowed off the leash. Elsewhere in the park, and throughout all provincial parks, pets must, of course, be leashed.

Joeperry Lake Trail

Hiking   Moderate   2 hours   6 km (return)

This linear trail ends at a small, semi-secluded beach on a quiet lake with no motorboat traffic.

BONNECHERE PROVINCIAL PARK

Box 220, Pembroke, Ontario K8A 6X4

Information: Call 613 757-2103
                      Fax   613 757-2295 (winter only)

Operating Season: May to October

Location: The park is off County Road 58 also known as Round Lake Road, 37 km southwest of Pembroke.

Natural features: The park takes its name from the Bonnechere River, once an important square timber logging route. The river meanders around several tiny oxbow lakes before reaching Round Lake.

There are three looped hiking trails in the park. Two are accessible from the main camping area, the third by crossing the Bonnechere River. All trails are a minimum of 0.5 m wide over an earth surface. Conducted nature walks are offered, and cross-country skiing and snowshoeing is available. Presently, the Beaver and Oxbow Trails are being reconstructed to make one trail which will be renamed the McNaughton Walk.

Beaver Marsh Trail

Hiking   Easy   45 minutes   1.5 km

The trail provides hikers with a view of a beaver marsh while winding through a mixed forest of maple, pine, cedar and white birch. There is access from the trail to a historic site called the Depot. The back section follows a gravel road before re-entering the forested trail.

Oxbow Trail

Hiking   Easy   1.5 hours   3 km

This combination looped and linear trail follows a gravel roadway 2.5 m wide with a 0.5-m-wide, looped section at its terminus. Secondary access is possible from the Beaver Marsh Trail. The forested loop section circles an old river oxbow.

Meandering River Nature Loop Trail

Hiking   Moderate   1 hour   2 km

This trail can be accessed by boat or canoe only. The route provides the hiker with opportunities to see mature trees, plants, animals and birds found in the park. There are some boardwalk sections along the trail.

CHARLESTON LAKE PROVINCIAL PARK

148 Woodvale Road, Lansdowne, Ontario K0E 1L0

Information: Call 613 659-2065

Operating season: May to October

Location: Take Exit 659 off Highway 401 east of Gananoque (east of Kingston). Travel north through the village of Lansdowne.

Natural features: The park sits on the Frontenac Axis, a southerly extension of the Precambrian Shield that divides the St. Lawrence Lowlands in two. This division gives rise to the Thousand Islands and the Adirondack Mountains of New York State. According to geologists, the area was once the boundary between two ancient bodies of water, Lake Iroquois to the southwest and the Champlain Sea to the east.

Black spruce bogs more typical of Northern Ontario can be found here beside more southern tree species such as pitch pine. Showy orchids, long-bracted orchid and shining sumac flourish here. The 194-m-high summit of Blue Mountain offers a fantastic view of the surrounding forest, lakes and farm country. There are some unusual rock formations which were once used as shelters by native peoples.

All the trails are 1.5 m wide and are composed of earth or wood chips. Four of the six trails are looped. Conducted nature walks are offered.

Sandstone Island Trail

Interpretive guide   Easy   2 hours   3.3 km

Travelling over a rolling terrain, the trail has 14 interpretive stops providing examples of the geological processes that created the landforms found in the park. In addition, hikers can see the rock shelters that were used by native peoples 2,000 years ago. The trail also passes by foundations of homesteads built by pioneers, and gives access to picturesque views from the top of the 8-m-high sandstone cliffs.

Shoreline Centennial Trail

Interpretive guide   Easy   1.5 hours   2 km

There are 14 stops explaining the natural and cultural history of the park and lake, especially the role of recreational fishing. Trail users are encouraged to bring along a lunch, as there are picnic facilities near the trail.

Tallow Rock Bay East Trail

Hiking   Moderate   2 hours   6 km (return)

This linear trail travels along the shoreline of the lake. There is an excellent swimming spot at the end.

Tallow Rock Bay West Trail

Hiking   Moderate   4–5 hours   14 km (return)

This linear trail has some boardwalk sections and travels through a variety of habitats including beaver ponds, large wildflower meadows and high rocky points. Views of the forest and lake and two spots for swimming are found along the trail.

Quiddity Trail

Hiking	Barrier-free	1.5 hours	2.6 km

The first 500 m section of this linear trail is barrier-free. The route passes over boardwalk sections through a swampy area, with frequent sightings of warblers, muskrats, painted turtles and wood ducks. The trail ends at a 35-m-high rocky lookout 35-m-high overlooking the lake.

Beechwoods Trail

Interpretive guide	Easy	1 hour	1.8 km

The trail goes through a stand of tall, mature beech trees. There are 12 interpretive stops for the hiker to read about the park's varied wildlife.

Hemlock Ridge Trail

Interpretive guide	Easy	1.5 hours	2 km

This trail passes through a mature hemlock forest and a forest drowned as a result of beaver activity. There are 13 interpretive stops that identify tree species and explain the forest community.

FERRIS PROVINCIAL PARK
Box 1409, Campbellford, Ontario K0L 1L0

Information   Call 705 653-3575 (summer)
               705 653-1566 (year round, Monday–Friday)
         Fax 705 653-5203

Operating season: May to October (off-season trail access is possible)

Location: The park is a short distance south of Campbellford on County Road 8, east of Peterborough.

Natural features: The park is situated on a series of rolling hills called drumlins which overlook the Trent River. Formed by till left behind by the glaciers once covering Ontario, these almond-shaped hills are the ideal spot for a panoramic view of the area. Stone fences and cleared meadows are relics of farms that were once worked here.

Ferris Trails

Hiking	Easy to Strenuous	1.5 hours	3 km

There are three interconnected trails, about 0.5 m wide, with mainly earth surfaces. The Blue Trail is a strenuous loop of 1.5 km, which travels over a glacial drumlin. The 1.0-km Yellow Trail is moderately difficult to walk, and travels along the Trent River ending at a viewing platform overlooking the Ranney Falls. The Red Trail — the easiest — is a half-kilometre loop following a roadway back to the start of the trail system.

FITZROY PROVINCIAL PARK
Fitzroy Harbour, Ontario K0A 1X0

Information: Call 613 623-5159

Operating season: May to October

Location: The park is situated along the Ottawa River, 12 km west of Highway 17, and 20 km north of Arnprior.

Natural features: As you walk or drive along the main park road, you'll notice that the land descends to terraces at the river's edge. These steps mark the former shores of the Ottawa River during and after the melting of the glaciers. There is a majestic forest of white pine and 300-year-old burr oak.

Both trails are looped, 1.5 m wide, travelling over an earth path. There are groomed cross-country ski trails available.

The Carp Trail

Hiking	Easy	30 minutes	1 km

The trail travels along the banks of the Carp River through a mature forest. There is a number of interconnecting trails which are well marked.

The Terraces Trail

Interpretive guide   Moderate   1 hour   1.6 km

The trail travels through a forest to a boulder field and areas of exposed bedrock. Stairs help trail users explore two levels of terraces. There are eight interpretive stops that explain the making of the terraces and surrounding landscape.

FRONTENAC PROVINCIAL PARK

Box 11, 1090 Salmon Lake Road, Sydenham, Ontario K0H 2T0

Information: Call 613 376-3489

Operating season: Open all year round

Location: The park is 45 km north of Kingston, and 12 km northeast of Sydenham, off Highway 38.

Natural features: The park terrain is rugged as it is situated on the Frontenac Axis, the southernmost part of the Canadian Shield. There are three distinct habitat areas. The first or northern area is rolling hills covered with stands of sugar maple and red oak and sprinkled with ponds and lakes. The second area of ridges, valleys and numerous lakes is covered in younger trees. The third or southern area is of bare rock ridges with numerous scattered bogs and marshes. Many rare plants grow here such as great-spurred violet, silvery glade fern, puddyroot and blunt-lobed woodsia fern.

All 11 trails are looped, a minimum of 0.5 m wide, travelling mostly over earth path and smooth rock. Many of the trails have boardwalk sections. Conducted nature walks are offered. Cross-country skiing and snowshoeing trails are provided. Remember to include additional hiking distances to the trailheads during winter due to the closure of Big Salmon Lake Road.

Arab Lake Gorge Trail

Interpretive guide   Easy   45 minutes   1.5 km

There are nine interpretive stops along the gorge to give visitors an excellent close-up look at the geology, flora and fauna.

Doe Lake Trail

| Hiking | Easy | 1–2 hours | 3 km |

The trail skirts three beaver ponds along the shore of South Otter Lake, climbing to a spectacular lookout over Doe Lake and returning through a forested area along its shore. It also explores some of the landforms found in the southern area of the park, and includes a side trail that leads to an early 19th-century mica mine.

Cedar Lake Trail

| Backpacking | Strenuous | 4–6 hours | 16.8 km |
| Map | | | |

The trail features the largest complex of wetlands in the park. It skirts Arab Lake and Doe Lake and passes by the lowland area of Cedar Lake.

Slide Lake Trail

| Hiking | Very strenuous | 7–9 hours | 30.2 km |

This looped trail, with views over lake and forest, is located in the most rugged part of the park. The trail passes a series of waterfalls which drop 16 m from Slide Lake to North Buck Lake. It features an excellent view of Mink and Camel Lakes and the ridge and trough landscape of the park. Parts of this trail join with the Rideau Trail. Use caution during the summer months as many parts of the trail cross over extensive barren rock outcrops which can get extremely hot or slippery.

Big Salmon Lake Trail

| Backpacking | Strenuous | 6–8 hours | 28 km |
| Map | | | |

The trail circles Big Salmon Lake, and features the shoreline forest and cliffs and includes several lookouts. The southern portion of the trail is more rugged and passes by a few early 19th-century homesteads near Black Lake and Little Clear Lake.

Arkon Lake Trail

| Hiking | Moderate | 3–5 hours | 16.8 km |

The trail features a bog, several beaver ponds and stages of forest growth from immature to mature. There is also a clear view of Arkon Lake.

Little Clear Lake Trail

Backpacking   Moderate   4–6 hours   24 km
Map

The trail provides access to several abandoned homestead sites, developed in the early 19th century in the area of Little Clear Lake.

Little Salmon Lake Trail

Hiking   Strenuous   5–6 hours   22 km
Backpacking/Map

The route takes you through a mature forest and around Little Salmon Lake and travels through Moulton Gorge, a deep valley in the centre of the park.

Tetsmine Lake Trail

Hiking   Strenuous   6–9 hours   31.2 km
Backpacking/Map

Hikers visit a landscape of marble ridges, rocky outcrops and mature deciduous forests. In addition, parts of an old log slide, abandoned mica mines and the remains of the McNally homestead on Kingsford Lake can be seen. This trail also includes an interesting view at the north end of Moulton Gorge.

Gibson Lake Trail

Backpacking   Strenuous   6–9 hours   34 km
Map

The Gibson Lake loop is a combination of the Gibson and Hemlock Trail loops. You should be aware that some hikers have found the route a little confusing. This trail takes you through a mature forest area and by an old log cabin near campsite 11.

Hemlock Lake Trail

Hiking   Moderate   2–4 hours   5 km

The hiker travels through a mature forest and an abandoned homestead field, and passes the site of an old logging shanty near Hemlock Lake.

Frontenac Park section of Rideau Trail

The Rideau Trail is a 300-km, long-distance hiking trail that runs between Kingston and Ottawa. The trail in this park is designated by an orange triangle and passes through the southern section. It shares sections of the Cedar and Slide Lake loops. It is recommended that you reserve campsites 1 and 2 when using this section of the trail.

LAKE ST. PETER PROVINCIAL PARK

Ministry of Natural Resources, Box 500, Bancroft, Ontario K0L 1C0

Information: Call 613 338-5312 (Park Office, May to October)

Operating season: Mid-May to October

Location: The park is situated off Highway 127, about 45 km north of Bancroft, and to the south of Algonquin Provincial Park.

Natural features: The park is on the southern edge of the Canadian Shield and the bedrock in the area contains many notable minerals. Trees such as white birch and white pine shelter mammals such as raccoons and chipmunks, moose and deer. Birds to look for include warblers, woodpeckers and the great blue heron.

There are two interconnected, looped hiking trails in the park. Both start and end at the same place. Signs along the trails identify some of the trees.

Lookout Trail

Hiking	Strenuous	1.5 hours	2.4 km

There are steep climbs and descents along this trail, and a resting bench is provided at a scenic lookout. The narrow trail allows for many large trees and wildflowers to grow close to the trail. The final section of the trail follows a paved park road.

Cabin Trail

Hiking	Strenuous	2 hours	4.3 km

This trail branches off the Lookout Trail just after the scenic lookout, then loops back to it. There are steep climbs and descents before the trail reaches the remains of an abandoned log cabin. Signs of moose and bear are found along the trail and there is a variety of birds. Towards the end of the hike there is a kettle pond, inhabited by an active beaver colony.

MURPHYS POINT PROVINCIAL PARK

R.R. 5, Perth, Ontario K7H 3C7

Information: Call 613 267-5060

Operating season: May to October
                  December to March

Location: The park is off County Road 21, 19 km south of Perth at the top of Big Rideau Lake.

Natural features: The park sits on the Frontenac Axis, a southern extension of the Canadian Shield, and used to be mined for minerals such as mica, feldspar and apatite. The forest is diverse with pockets of maples, oak and beech amongst white pine ridges. A number of rare species, including the black rat snake, are found here. A restored turn-of-the-century mine, a ruined sawmill, and pioneer homesteads are some of the historical features of the park.

All six trails are a minimum of 0.5 m wide, travelling over earth path and rock. Conducted nature walks are offered. Other trail activities include mountain biking and cross-country skiing.

Silver Queen Mine Trail*

Interpretive displays   Easy   1 hour   2 km

This looped trail leads to a historic mica mine site. There are seven interpretive display panels telling the story of the mine. In addition, there are scheduled tours of the abandoned underground mine and its facilities.

*Al's Picks, see page 133.

Sylvan Trail

| Hiking | Strenuous | 1.5 hours | 2.5 km |

The trail winds through a deciduous forest of beech, sugar maple and oak before looping back to the beginning.

Point Trail

| Hiking | Moderate | 2 hours | 4 km |

This trail winds through the forest along the shoreline of Big Rideau Lake. There is an excellent picnic spot with an open view of the lake on the peninsula known as Murphys Point.

Beaver Pond Trail

| Hiking | Moderate | 1.5 hours | 2.5 km (return) |

This linear trail travels along the top of an old beaver dam and beside the pond that the dam created.

Prospectors' Trail

| Hiking | Easy | 20 minutes | 0.5 km |

This looped trail has some grades but steps are provided. There are trail-side views of a series of test pits. These pits were dug by miners who were prospecting for minerals.

McParlan Trail

| Hiking | Easy | 1 hour | 2.5 km (return) |

Following the shoreline of Hogg Bay this linear trail travels past the mouth of Black Creek, the McParlan house and ruins of the Burgess Sawmill.

Section of Rideau Trail

| Hiking | Moderate | 2.5 hours | 6.5 km |

This linear, 0.5-m-wide earth path is part of the Rideau long-distance hiking trail. This trail is 385 km long (including side trails) extending from Kingston on

Lake Ontario to Chaudiere Falls on the Ottawa River near Ottawa. This section of the Rideau Trail, which runs through the park, is indicated by orange triangular markers. It passes through meadows and along a beaver pond. A guidebook for the trail is available.

PRESQU'ILE PROVINCIAL PARK
R.R. 4, Brighton, Ontario K0K 1H0

Information: Call 613 475-4324

Operating Season: All year

Location: The park is reached from Highway 401 just a short distance south of Brighton. It is 155 km east of Toronto.

Natural features: The park is a boomerang-shaped spit of sand and limestone that juts sharply 10 km into Lake Ontario. The land formation is a tombolo, created as wind and waves piled sand and gravel from the lake bottom between a limestone island and the mainland. The action of the water and wind reinforces the peninsula with sand and causes the beach to grow by as much as 2 m each year. The park includes a variety of environments such as sand dunes, forests, and reedy marshes. The coastal wet meadows (pannes) are internationally known.

The park is a haven for migratory birds. About 126 species have nested here, and at least 317 species have been sighted en route for destinations in South America, Africa and Europe. Shorebirds are also plentiful along the beaches and can be observed from the Natural Beach Trail. Waterfowl thrive in the marshes and can be seen from the interpretive Marsh Boardwalk Trail. Each autumn, the park is a gathering point for monarch butterflies before they take off on their migration south.

All the trails are a minimum of 1.0 m wide travelling over an earth path. There is a park tabloid (information sheet) illustrating all the trails. Conducted nature walks are offered. A cycling trail is available and two hiking trails are used for cross-country skiing.

Marsh Boardwalk Trail*

Interpretive displays Easy   1 hour   1.2 km

This looped trail has ten interpretive signs along its length to describe the rich aquatic, vegetative, and bird life living in the marsh. Visitors have an opportunity to observe the living marsh just beside the boardwalk, and to see a variety of waterfowl and birds. The majority of the trail is level boardwalk, with viewing platforms and resting areas provided. The last 400 m of trail are located on land, meandering through an interesting forest stand of white cedar. At points along this stretch of the land trail, access is restricted to less than a metre. Visitors in wheelchairs would probably need assistance to get through these narrow spots.

*Al's Picks, see page 135.

Jobes Nature Trail

Interpretive guide   Easy   1 hour   1.2 km

This level, looped trail has a variety of walking surfaces ranging from earth path, wood chips and boardwalk. A short section is constructed of logs laid side by side. This section of the trail is difficult to walk on, and care should be taken. There are plans to have these logs removed and replaced with boardwalk. There are 13 interpretive stops along the trail explaining the forest ecology. The trail leads you through mature stands of yellow birch, eastern hemlock, sugar maple and stripped maple. Of special note is an abundance of ferns (25 species) and the presence of plants typical of the Atlantic Coastal Plains such as tubercled orchid. Many of these plants can be seen from the trail itself.

Newcastle Trail

Hiking   Easy   2 hours   3.5 km

This linear trail leads from the campground to the Presqu'ile lighthouse. There is one steep grade. The trail travels through a variety of habitats such as old field succession, old-growth forests and old sand dune areas. One section of this trail creates a loop and follows an abandoned asphalt roadway offering barrier-free use. Pileated woodpeckers are often visible near the trail.

Natural Beach Trail

| Hiking | Easy | 1 hour | 1.2 (return) |

There have been up to 38 species of shorebird observed along this linear trail, during migration periods in spring and fall. From three non-disruptive designated viewing areas visitors may see species such as ring-billed gull, double-crested cormorant, and caspian and common terns. As well, Gull and High Bluff Islands, located just off-shore, supply nesting habitat for colonies of water birds.

SANDBANKS PROVINCIAL PARK
R.R. 1, Picton, Ontario K0K 2T0

Information: Call 613 393-3319

Operating season: May to October

Location: The park is south of Belleville on the Lake Ontario shore of Prince Edward County. Take Highway 62 south to County Road 12.

Natural features: Two spectacular stretches of sand dunes make this park unique and memorable. These include the West Lake formation, considered the largest freshwater sand dune system in the world. Many of the dunes are between 12 m and 25 m high.

Some of the unusual plants found in the park are bluets, horary puccoon, sea rocket and sand spurge. The open dunes have pine, maple and cedar growing in abundance. Some of the wildlife includes songbirds such as white-throated sparrow, marsh wren and swamp sparrow, and mammals such as fox and deer and several types of reptiles and amphibians.

A new trail was constructed in 1998 for the West Lake dunes area. Conducted nature walks are offered.

Cedar Sands Trail

| Interpretive guide | Easy | 1 hour | 2 km |

This looped, 1.0-m-wide earth trail has stairways to access the sensitive sand dune area. There are 12 interpretive stops explaining the ecology of a dune forest and two viewing platforms overlooking the Outlet River and the Baymouth sand dune system.

SHARBOT LAKE PROVINCIAL PARK

R.R. 2, Sharbot Lake, Ontario K0H 2P0

Information: Call 613 335-2814

Operating season: May to September

Location: The park is on Highway 7, about 30 km west of Perth, southwest of Ottawa.

Natural features: The park's landscape supports a diverse, mixed forest of maple, oak, birch, butternut and hickory. Red ash, sumac, cedar, and hemlock grow on top of the rocky ridges that rise abruptly above the lakeshore. Flowering plants include sarsparilla, trillium, hepatica and Solomon's seal. Much rarer are Indian pipes (a saprophytic), ladies' tresses (an orchid) and delicate maiden fern.

Both trails are 0.5 m wide, travelling over an earth path and smooth rock.

Ridgeview Trail

| Hiking | Easy | 45 minutes | 0.5 km (return) |

This linear trail passes through a deciduous forest to the top of a ridge. A viewing lookout provides an impressive view of Black and Sharbot Lakes. There is one steep climb to access the top of the ridge.

Discovery Trail

| Interpretive displays | Easy | 1 hour | 1.2 km |

This looped trail takes you to a pleasant view of Sharbot Lake. There are ten display panels to explain the geology and ecology of the Canadian Shield.

SILENT LAKE PROVINCIAL PARK

Box 500, Bancroft, Ontario K0L 1C0

Information: Call 613 339-2807
613 332-3940 (October to April)

Operating season: Open all year

Location: The park is on Highway 28 about 25 km north of Apsley and 24 km south of Bancroft.

Natural features: The forest is a mix of deciduous and evergreen trees, with white birch, maple, hemlock and white pine being the most common species. A wide variety of wildflowers grows throughout the park, including a rare rose, pogonia, rattlesnake fern and toothwort. Otter, mink and beaver live in the marshy areas near the shoreline of the lake, and deer can often be seen on the higher ground.

There are three short looped hiking trails, 1.5 m wide, travelling over an earth path and rock surface. Conducted nature walks are offered. There are three mountain bike trails, four cross-country ski trails, and one snowshoeing trail. A publication entitled "A Guide to the Trails of Silent Lake Provincial Park" is available.

Lakehead Loop Trail

| Hiking | Easy | 30 minutes | 1.5 km |

This trail provides a gentle walk along the Silent Lake shoreline through cedar and black ash trees to a point overlooking an island in the lake. The trail returns along higher ground through stands of hemlock, sugar maple and red oak trees. It narrows to 0.5 m in width and has some steep grades.

Bonnie's Pond Trail

| Hiking | Moderate | 1.5 hours | 3 km |

Passing through a meadow, the trail winds beneath mature beech trees, and hikers may spot chipmunks, squirrels, mink, beaver and otter. Eventually the trail reaches a spectacular lookout point close to the end of the trail.

Lakeshore Hiking Trail

Hiking   Strenuous   4–6 hours   15 km

This trail follows the undeveloped shoreline of Silent Lake. It is rugged, challenging and rewarding. The hiker will travel through beaver meadows, hardwood forests, and cedar and black ash swamps. There are colourful rock cuts, sparkling mineral crystals and granite outcrops. A short distance from the beginning brings the hiker to a spectacular lookout point. The trail can also be accessed at various points by canoe.

SILVER LAKE PROVINCIAL PARK
R.R. 2, Maberly, Ontario K0H 2B0

Operating season: May to September

Information: Call 613 268-2000

Location: This park is on Highway 7, 12 km west of Perth, and 10 km east of Sharbot Lake.

Natural features: In past millenia, glaciers funnelled through here, scraping away the soil. The thin soil discouraged farmers but heartened prospectors seeking iron, mica, quartz, feldspar, and semi-precious stones. By the early part of this century, some 45 mines had been established within a 16-km radius of Silver Lake.

The forests consist of young maple and ironwood saplings, and mature mixed hardwood trees of maple, basswood, eastern hemlock, oak, elm and black ash. Ground vegetation includes goldenthread, winterberry, sensitive fern and wild sarsparilla. A wide variety of wildlife lives in the park.

Marsh Trail

Hiking   Easy   30 minutes   0.5 km (return)

This linear trail is 1.0 m wide and travels over an earth path, gravel and boardwalk section along a marsh area and over to a small island. A variety of marsh plant life can be readily seen from the boardwalk.

VOYAGEUR PROVINCIAL PARK

Box 130, Chute-a-Blondeau, Ontario K0B 1B0

Information: Call 613 674-2825

Operating season: May to October
December to March

Location: The park is one hour's drive east of Ottawa, off Highway 417, at Exit 5, near Hawkesbury and the Quebec and U.S. borders.

Natural features: The park is situated on the shores of the Ottawa River. Here the fertile soil of the St. Lawrence Lowlands meets the ancient bedrock of the Canadian Shield. This varied landscape provides an ideal habitat for beaver, deer and a variety of birds such as meadowlarks and warblers. Shorebirds and waterfowl stop here temporarily during migration.

Conducted nature walks are offered. There are equestrian and cross-country ski trails available.

Coureurs du Bois Trail

Interpretive displays   Easy   1 hour   2.5 km

This looped, 1.0-m-wide earth path and boardwalk trail traverses a glacial moraine to a beaver pond. There are two steep grades. There are ten display panels along the trail describing the area's habitats and geology.

Outouais Trail

Hiking   Easy   2 hours   5 km (return)

This linear 2-m-wide earth path and boardwalk trail provides access to a variety of park facilities such as beaches and campgrounds.

Equestrian Trail

Hiking   Moderate   2 hours   6 km

This looped, 0.5-m-wide earth trail explores a mature forest. There are four long steep grades and it's shared with horseback riders.

AL'S PICKS

Murphys Point Provincial Park: The Silver Queen Mine Trail

Starting at the historic Lally Homestead parking lot, this delightfully easy walk leads you to an abandoned mine site. It is significant because it is a good example of the small-scale mining that occurred on the Canadian Shield during the early 1900s. Interpretive display panels along the trail describe its heart-rending story, and point out remains of structures that relate to the early miners and settlers of the area. This section follows a level, wide, hard-packed road ideal for a child's stroller until it reaches the trail itself, leading to the mine.

The first part of the trail runs through an abandoned farm pasture slowly reverting to a forest. An old wooden wagon beside the trail reminds the visitor of the hardships encountered by the early settlers. Trees of maple, basswood and oak grow along the perimeter of the fields and the grassy pastureland is the perfect place to catch sight of one of a variety of songbirds like the black-billed cuckoo, bluebird and yellow warbler. The road soon closes in with a young deciduous forest that has taken over the piles of waste rock from the mine, and is growing on both sides of the roadway.

By now the interpretive panels along the trail should have whetted your appetite and curiosity about the Silver Queen Mine. To appreciate more fully the workings of a mica mine and the life of an early miner, consider taking a guided

Inside the Silver Queen Mine cavern with a nature guide.

interpretive tour of the old mine and learn first-hand about its operation. The interpretive program takes the visitor into a huge cavern 20 m high with walls sparkling with mica and visits the restored bunkhouse near the mine that has been turned into a museum displaying mine artifacts.

At the mine site another trail, called the Prospector Trail has recently been incorporated into the Silver Queen Mine Trail. This short but rugged looped trail takes you alongside small open-pit mineral mines. When you return from the mine site, you can either retrace your steps along the same trail or you can take an alternate route back along the rugged Beaver Pond Trail. This trail travels along the top of an abandoned beaver dam, giving you an idea of how beaver dams are constructed. Watch closely as you might see a beaver in the pond or near its lodge. Choosing either trail will lead you back to the start of the trail within half an hour.

Bon Echo Provincial Park: The Shield Trail

Just past the park entrance is the Shield Trail. This introductory hike to the Canadian Shield environment has something for nearly everyone. For the amateur botanist there is all the plant life found along the trail and in the marshes, while for the history buff it's a chance to walk along the abandoned historic Addington roadway, used in the late 19th century by early settlers and loggers. The trail leaves the roadway following a well-marked wilderness route designed to give you an idea of the land that greeted those first settlers.

As you walk along it is clear that nature has concealed almost all evidence of the presence of humans. However, glimpses of old logging operations, mining sites and agriculture help the imagination to provide evidence of the early settlers. A 45-minute walk beyond the end of the abandoned roadway takes you to remnants of the white pine that once covered large sections of this area. Lumbermen and settlers moved into the Shield area and removed the magnificent trees, and other events, such as fire, changed the forest. In spite of these events, the forest through which you now walk has almost regained wilderness stature.

The trail continues through a mature mixed forest around the side of a small marsh. Smooth rock outcrops surround the marsh where you can rest and watch for wildlife to appear. A short distance from here, is an old beaver dam that has lost almost all its water. Along the shoreline you will find sundew, lady's slippers and even the hoof prints of deer.

By now you have travelled for about two hours with 20 more minutes before you return to the start of the trail. You will start to get glimpses of tranquil Bon Echo Lake through the trees on your left, and as the trail turns towards the lake you will be able to see that its shores are steep and lined with Labrador tea shrubs. There are openings in the trees along the shoreline, and you might want to stop for lunch or just enjoy the loons that may swim by. The trailhead is ten minutes away.

Presqui'le Provincial Park: Marsh Boardwalk Trail

There is something about walking on a boardwalk that is enjoyable for everyone. The Presqu'ile Marsh Boardwalk Trail provides a solid, wide and accessible trail allowing for easy travelling through the largest protected marsh on the north shore of Lake Ontario. The trail starts at a parking lot and within two minutes' walking arrives at the beginning of the boardwalk and the first of two viewing platforms. This platform is equipped with ramps for wheelchairs, as well as rest benches.

In the spring, bald eagles can be seen anywhere along the boardwalk and the distinctive songs of the red-winged blackbird and swamp sparrow can be heard. Sometimes the extraordinary whirring song of the pied-billed grebe or belted kingfisher fills the air, lending an almost jungle-like sound. During an evening walk, you will be surrounded by the loud and clear sounds of the spring peeper and chorus frogs.

In the summer, you are never alone as you walk. The marsh is teeming with insect life. Many different dragonflies and damselflies can be seen patrolling the marsh. Huge bullfrogs and shiny green frogs are numerous, while painted and snapping turtles can be seen sunning themselves on logs close to the boardwalk. It is common to see wading birds such as great blue heron, green-backed heron and black-crowned night heron strolling around in the marsh or standing perfectly still waiting for a meal to swim by. Showy, fragrant, white water lilies float on the surface of the water, opening only from mid-morning to early afternoon. Or you may see the abundant blue-purple iris, whose name in Greek means "goddess of the rainbow."

An extra bonus of this trail is the opportunity it provides in the fall to see the thousands of migrating songbirds and waterfowl close-up. You can watch up to 50,000 roosting swallows getting ready for their flight south, or try to identify the more than 30 species of waterfowl such as mallards, blue- and green-winged teal and wood ducks as they gather before their long southerly flight. The muskrat will be even more noticeable as the cattails have died. It is a common sight swimming past or under the boardwalk on its way to its home in the mound of cattail roots.

After a short walk down the trail you enter the dense clumps of cattails in the marsh and arrive at the first of ten colourful interpretive stops strategically placed along the boardwalk to give information on some of the plants and wildlife living nearby.

The last viewing platform is a tower, 45 minutes' walk from the trail's beginning. It offers a spectacular panorama of the entire marsh. Be sure to bring your binoculars and camera. Shortly after leaving the tower, the boardwalk ends and the last 300 m of trail are over land. You travel through a stand of eastern white cedar with unusually twisted and contorted trunks, the result of their having to compete for the sunlight.

SOUTHWESTERN REGION

PARKS OF THE REGION

Awenda
Bronte Creek
Earl Rowe
John E. Pearce
MacGregor Point

Pinery
Point Farms
Port Burwell
Rock Point
Rondeau

Sauble Falls
Selkirk
Springwater
Turkey Point
Wasaga Beach

AWENDA PROVINCIAL PARK

Box 5004, Penetanguishene, Ontario L9M 2G2

Information: Call 705 549-2231
                       Fax 705 549-4792

Operating season: May to October

Location: The park is located at the tip of the Penetanguishene peninsula on southern Georgian Bay. It is a 25-minute drive from the Penetanguishene-Midland area.

Natural features: The most prominent geomorphic feature of the park is the Nipissing Bluff, which rises 60 m above the Georgian Bay shoreline, and runs for the entire length of the park. Glacial remnants such as cobble and sand beaches, erratics, kettle lakes, sand dunes, post-glacial fossil beach terraces, and a glacial spillway may be seen within the park. On top of the bluff, a forest of American beech and sugar maple dominates. Below the bluff lies a lowland forest of eastern hemlock and yellow birch with pockets of white cedar and specked alder. The fall colours are spectacular.

Many different types of birds can be found in the park with over 200 bird species having been recorded, including 29 kinds of warbler. Thirty-two reptile and amphibian species have been identified. Awenda also has a rich cultural heritage. There are several significant First Nations' archaeological sites.

There are seven trails clearly marked in the park. All the trails have a minimum width of 1.0 m and most travel over an earth path. Four of the trails are linear. Conducted nature walks are offered. A park tabloid (information sheet) in French and English has a map of all the trails. Other trail activities available are mountain biking and cross-country skiing.

Beaver Pond Trail

Interpretive display   Barrier-free   30 minutes   1 km

This loop travels over a limestone fines surface and a boardwalk. It circles an active beaver pond. Remnants of a bridge and logging building are nearby. There are five interpretive display panels detailing some of the cultural, geographical and natural features along the trail.

Beach Trail

| Hiking | Easy | 1.25 hours | 4 km (return) |

This trail travels over an earth path and unpaved road by the side of Georgian Bay. When it reaches a black ash swamp, the contrast between dry oak-maple forest and wet birch-cedar forest is highlighted. There is an observation deck located near the beginning of the trail.

Brulé Trail

| Hiking | Easy | 1.25 hours | 4 km (return) |

Passing through a section of upland deciduous forest, the trail accesses some of the largest white pine, red oak and large-toothed aspen stands in the park. This area was logged in the late 1800s.

Bluff Trail

| Hiking | Moderate | 3.5 hours | 13 km |

This looped trail has a steep grade accessed by a 155-step stairway. The trail travels partly along a high bluff, and partly through a low wetland. It also covers a pine plantation and sand dune area.

Nipissing Trail

| Hiking | Moderate | 30 minutes | 1 km (return) |

There is one major steep grade. A stairway with 155 steps takes you to the top of the bluff providing a panoramic view of the forest canopy. The Bluff Trail connects here and they both use the same stairway. The trail travels through a lowland forest of cedar and white birch, eventually entering an upland forested area of maple and oak.

Dunes Trail

| Hiking | Easy | 1 hour | 3 km (return) |

The trail starts off with a steep grade up the Algonquin Bluff, a 12,000-year-old, post-glacial cliff rising 90 m above the Georgian Bay shoreline. The trail quickly levels off and leads to a sand dune area. Beside the trail are the remnants of two early homesteads.

Wendat Trail

| Hiking | Easy | 2 hours | 5 km |

The trail loops around a glacial kettle lake. Trail users can see an array of wildlife, including the great blue heron, common loon, snapping turtle and beaver. The trail passes through marsh and upland forest communities. Remnants of the Brabant homestead are present near the trail as well as a pine and spruce plantation.

BRONTE CREEK PROVINCIAL PARK
1219 Burloak Drive, Burlington, Ontario L7R 3X5

Information: Call 905 827-6911
Fax 905 637-4120

Operating season: Open all year

Location: The park is situated between Burlington and Oakville. Off the Queen Elizabeth Way, take the Burloak Drive exit, not Bronte Road.

Natural features: A wide stream from which Bronte Creek Park got its name flows through the park. Much of the land was used for agriculture, but since it became a park, it is regaining its natural cover of trees and plants. Most small mammals common to Southern Ontario live in the park, as well as some larger species, such as white-tailed deer and red fox. Birds in the park include the blue jay, red-tailed hawk and the occasional pileated and red-headed woodpecker, turkey vulture and short- and long-eared owls. As many as 20 amphibian and reptile species, more than 70 kinds of moths and butterflies and 125 species of insect, including a rare katydid have been recorded in the park's inventory.

Forty hectares in the park are devoted to an operating farm that reflects the way of life around 1900. Costumed park heritage interpreters perform old-fashioned domestic chores in a big Victorian farmhouse filled with period furniture. Several barns, chicken coops, an icehouse, and a woodshed have been restored on original foundations. Another farm area in the park invites children to climb and swing in a hayloft, or make friends with a variety of domesticated animals.

Three of the park's five trails are barrier-free. All the trails are 1.5 m to 2.5 m wide. Most are looped trails. Conducted nature walks and school tours are offered. Other trail uses are fitness training, cross-country skiing and mountain-biking.

Mice, Men and Maiden's Blush Trail

Interpretive guide   Barrier-free   1 hour   1 km

This trail travels over an earth path and compacted gravel surface, primarily through a deciduous forested area near a pond. There are opportunities to observe birds and small mammals. Using the trail guide, the ten interpretive stops explain the logging and urban farming that occurred in the area.

Half Moon Valley Trail*

Interpretive guide   Easy   1.5 hours   2 km

The trail, which travels primarily over gravel and boardwalk surfaces, includes three stairways on some steep sections. The route leads you through forested and bog areas to a lookout point at the creek. Using the trail guide, the 12 stops explain the signs of the area's human and glacial effects.

*Al's Picks, see page 161.

Trillium Trail

Hiking   Barrier-free   45 minutes   1 km

Well known for the abundance of wildflowers, especially trilliums in the spring, this wide, compacted gravel trail allows easy access. Each year a special Mother's Day Wildflower Festival is held to celebrate the arrival of spring flowers.

Logging Trail

Interpretive display   Barrier-free   45 minutes   1.2 km (return)

This 2.5-m-wide linear trail travels over earth and compacted gravel. There are three interpretive signs explaining trees and wildlife in the area. The woodlot area has been logged and forest management techniques are demonstrated.

Ravine Trail

Hiking   Easy   1.5 hours   2.7 km (return)

This linear trail travels over earth and gravel to a spectacular view of the whole ravine from a lookout platform. The ravine/river system has been documented as one of the least disturbed on the north shore of Lake Ontario. A sign explains the effects of the ravine on the vegetation.

EARL ROWE PROVINCIAL PARK
Box 872, Alliston, Ontario L9R 1W1

Information: Call 705 435-2498
                      Fax 705 435-4333

Operating season: May to September

Location: The park is located halfway between Lake Ontario and Georgian Bay near the town of Alliston. Take Highway 89 west, off Highway 400.

Natural features: The park is in the middle of characteristic south-central Ontario countryside. It includes a variety of valley landforms created by the meandering Boyne River. More than 100 bird species have been found here, including the ruby-throated hummingbird, yellow warbler and purple finch.

Three of the trails are linear. All trails are 1.5 m wide. With the exception of the barrier-free trail, all travel over earth path and meadows. Conducted nature walks are offered. Some of the trails can be used by mountain bikers.

The Lookout Trail

Interpretive guide   Moderate   1.5 hours   4 km

This looped trail has one very steep climb reaching a viewing platform with a spectacular view of the surrounding landscape. There is a guide with 11 interpretive stops that discuss the natural and cultural features of the area.

Resource Trail

Interpretive displays Easy   45 minutes   1.5 km (return)

The trail meanders alongside the Boyne River, through a marsh and into mature woodlands. Interpretive display panels explain some of the area's unique flora and fauna.

Fletcher's Pond Trail

Hiking	Barrier-free	45 minutes	1 km (return)

This paved trail starts at the main day use area and leads to the park's water reservoir, created by a dam on the Boyne River.

Little Trail

Interpretive displays	Easy	45 minutes	1 km (return)

The trail follows the shoreline of the water reservoir. There is a dam at the downstream end, where a fish ladder has been constructed to allow rainbow trout to pass upstream. Information on the fish ladder is provided.

JOHN E. PEARCE PROVINCIAL PARK
Box 9, Port Burwell, Ontario N0J 1T0

Information: Call 519 874-4691
                  Fax 519 874-4104

Operating season: June to October

Location: The park is on Lake Erie about 25 km southwest of St.Thomas and 5 km south of Wallacetown, off Highway 3.

Natural features: This small park has several rare Carolinian tree and plant species. The steep cliffs, 33 m high, provide fine viewing for gulls, diving ducks and other water birds. In the spring, wildflowers include red and white trilliums, blue cohosh, bloodroot and wild ginger.

The trail is located opposite the main entrance to the park. Conducted nature walks are offered.

Spicer Trail

Interpretive displays	Easy	1 hour	1.5 km

This trail starts as a linear trail, has a short loop at one end, and is 1.0 m wide on an earth path. There are 15 stops identifying large mature tree species, among the impressive mixture of young and old-growth Carolinian trees that surround the trail.

MACGREGOR POINT PROVINCIAL PARK

R.R. 1, Port Elgin, Ontario N0H 2C5

Information: Call 519 389-9056
Fax 519 388-9057

Operating season: May to October

Location: The park is on the shores of Lake Huron, south of Port Elgin in Bruce County, just west of Highway 21.

Natural features: The park's woodlands, silver maple swamps, cattail marshes, ponds, fens and sphagnum bogs all support a variety of plants, wildflowers and animals. A stop at Pitcher Plant Marl gives visitors a chance to see carnivorous plants. In the spring, the rare dwarf lake iris, or the elusive spotted turtle, may be seen. There are many opportunities to see such wildlife as deer, beaver, fox and porcupine. More than 200 species of bird have been sighted here, including the black-crowned night heron and American egret.

There are five trails between 1.0 m and 2 m wide. Most of the trails allow cycling and hiking together. There are no trail guides available, but a park information sheet (tabloid) provides a trail map, and some of the trails have interpretive display panels. Conducted nature walks are offered. There are mountain biking and cross-country skiing trails available in the park.

Lake Ridge Trail

Interpretive displays   Moderate   1.5 hours   4 km

This looped trail travels over boulders, earth, gravel and boardwalk. There are a few short steep grades. One of the main features is an active beaver pond about halfway along. Other features are the remains of a corduroy logging road, and of early settlers' plantings such as lilac and apple trees. There are nine interpretive storyboards explaining a variety of natural and historical features found along the trail.

Huron Fringe Trail

Interpretive displays   Barrier-free   45 minutes   1.2 km

This loop starts at the Visitors' Centre and features a level boardwalk surface. There are seven interpretive display boards to explain how the extremes in temperature dictate which plants grow on the sand dunes, as well as how the wetlands were formed and what animals and plants you might see in the ponds and surrounding area.

The Ducks Unlimited Trail

Hiking   Easy   1.5 hours   3.5 km (return)

This linear trail travels over compacted gravel and boardwalk, to a cairn near a control dam. This dam was built in partnership with Ducks Unlimited. The wetlands that have been created are used by ducks such as mallards, teal and wood ducks, as well as herons, beaver, muskrat and turtles. A viewing tower is provided for a sweeping view over the wetland. The trail, which is being expanded, passes through a cedar forest and a series of ponds.

Kempf's Trail

Hiking   Easy   30 minutes   1.6 km (return)

This linear trail travels over compacted limestone fines and follows a former shoreline. It is a link from the Old Shore Road Trail to the Ducks Unlimited Trail. Some small wetlands may be seen from the trail.

Old Shore Road Trail

Hiking   Easy   2 hours   6 km

This 3.5-m-wide, linear trail travels over a hard road bed of compacted gravel, as well as over earth with some sections of boardwalk next to the Lake Huron shoreline. The trail offers excellent views of the shore and beach areas. Viewing platforms are located in several places such as Watersnake Pond and Pitcher Plant Marl. The trail can be accessed from a number of points. Time and distance indicated is based on one-way travel along its length.

PINERY PROVINCIAL PARK
R.R. 2, Grand Bend, Ontario N0M 1T0

Information: Call 519 243-2220
              Fax 519-243-3851

Operating season: Open all year

Location: The park is on Lake Huron 6 km south of Grand Bend on Highway 21, about 50 km northeast of Sarnia.

Pinery Provincial Park.

Natural features: Spectacular sand dunes, meadows and a rare oak savannah are found in the park. Rarer than the rain forest, the oak savannah ecosystem grows within the sand dune landscape of the park. Oaks preside over a mosaic of prairie grasses, wildflowers, shrubs and meadows.

There have been over 700 plants and 300 bird species recorded. The blue heart, found in the park's wet meadows, grows only in a few other Canadian locations. Another rare prairie plant is the dense, blazing star. The park is home to 30 mammal species and 60 types of butterflies.

Many of the trail surfaces are limestone screenings. This material is fine limestone rock, heavily compacted, and it creates a very comfortable walking surface. All the trails are looped and about 1.0 m wide. Cycling and cross-country skiing trails are available. There are conducted walks and school tours offered.

Bittersweet Trail

Interpretive guide   Easy   1 hour   1.5 km

The trail travels through a mature oak and pine forest to the banks of the Old Ausable River Channel. There are a couple of short steep grades. There are 11 interpretive stops, and the guide offers insight into the varied lives of the park's mammals.

Carolinian Trail

Interpretive guide   Easy   1 hour   1.8 km

The trail travels along a sand dune ridge that overlooks the Ausable floodplain; there are some steep grades, but wooden stairs are provided, as are benches and viewing platforms. There are 11 interpretive stops. The guide describes the ecology of the Carolinian Forest.

Cedar Trail

Interpretive guide   Barrier-free   1 hour   2.3 km

Passing through the park's rare and expansive oak savannah community, the trail has ten interpretive stops to explore aspects of this unique habitat. Benches and sections of boardwalk are provided. A 1.0-km extension (not barrier-free) offers access to the shore of Lake Huron.

Heritage Trail*

Interpretive guide   Barrier-free   1.5 hours   2.5 km

This trail meanders through the park's extensive oak savannah to the banks of the Ausable River Channel. There are 12 stops referring to the full colour trail guide, which highlight times, events or the roles of individuals in the history of the park. A 0.6-km extension leads to a boardwalk, viewing platform and canoe dock overlooking the Old Ausable Channel. This takes about 15 minutes to walk.

*Al's Picks, see page 163.

Hickory Trail

Interpretive displays   Easy   45 minutes   1 km

The trail skirts the Ausable River. There are seven interpretive panel displays. Watch for the ragged bark of the shagbark hickory and the seed pods of bladdernut while observing the diversity of other plants along the trail.

Lookout Trail

Interpretive displays   Easy   1 hour   1 km

Along the trail six interpretive displays explain the variety of natural habitats. The trail ascends one of the park's highest sand dunes via a long stairway, where there is an excellent view of the Thedford Bog and the surrounding area.

Nipissing Trail

Interpretive displays   Easy   1 hour   2 km

This trail leads you to the park's oldest and largest dune ridge affording a view of most of the park, Lake Huron and adjacent farmland. Special notice should be taken of the new plant growth after a controlled burn in 1993. There are some steep grades with wooden stairs to climb. Eight interpretive display panels explain an oak savannah community.

Pine Trail

Interpretive displays   Easy   45 minutes   0.8 km

The trail passes through a dense stand of red pines. Six interpretive display panels explain the difference between the oak savannah found here and the forest in the rest of the park. There are some steep grades, but wooden stairs are provided.

Riverside Trail

Interpretive guide   Barrier-free   45 minutes   1 km

This trail includes benches, boardwalk and a viewing platform. It passes from a dry upland oak and pine forest to the Ausable River floodplain. There are 12 interpretive stops, each one discussing a unique aspect of the Ausable River's natural community. The trail is perfect for observing bird and wildlife in the park.

Wilderness Trail

Interpretive guide   Easy   1.5 hours   3 km

The trail passes through some of the park's oldest growth of red pine and mixed oak and pine forest, eventually reaching the shores of Lake Huron. There are 12 interpretive stops, each explaining part of the life cycle of a tree in particular as well as the park's oak and pine habitat in general.

POINT FARMS PROVINCIAL PARK
R.R. 3, Goderich, Ontario N7A 3X9

Information: Call 519 524-7124
              Fax   519 243-3851

Operating season: May to October

Location: The park is 6 km north of Goderich off Highway 21, on Lake Huron.

Natural features: The park is perched atop a steep bluff on the Lake Huron shoreline, and offers a panoramic view of the lake, 25 m below. Open fields broken by hedgerows and orchards are evidence of former farms. Various stages of plant succession can be observed, from open grassy fields to dense dogwood. A small woodlot of sugar maple, elm and beech provides habitat for wildlife. In the spring and fall there is a good chance that hikers will see migratory birds such as bobolink and the rufous-sided towhee.

There are three interconnected trails which are not clearly marked. They are looped, 1.5 m wide, leading over an earth and grass path. The guide is displayed on the park tabloid (information sheet). Conducted nature hikes are offered. Park roads are used for snowshoeing and cross-country skiing.

The Old Farms Trail

Interpretive guide   Easy   1 hour   3 km

The trail starts at the Visitors' Centre and has nine stops along the way explaining native tree species and the history of the park.

Below the Bluff Trail

Interpretive guide   Easy   1 hour   2 km

This section of the trail is a continuation of the Ravine Trail. It skirts Lake Huron, then follows a section of roadway climbing to the top of the bluff. There is a steady, steep climb, with six stops discussing the tree species.

Ravine Trail

Interpretive guide   Easy   30 minutes   1 km

This trail is reached from the Old Farm Trail. Four interpretive stops discuss the native plants and trees growing near the trail. Use caution during wet weather as it can be slippery.

PORT BURWELL PROVINCIAL PARK

Box 9, Port Burwell, Ontario N0J 1T0

Information: Call 519 874-4691
              Fax 519 874-4104

Operating season: May to October

Location: Near Port Burwell, 26 km south of Tillsonburg (take Highway 19) on the Lake Erie shore.

Natural features: The park lies on a natural formation known as the Norfolk Sand Plain. Erosion of this sand plain by Lake Erie is responsible for the park's 2-km-long beach and impressive shore bluffs. More than 85 kinds of migratory birds have been spotted here. Small sections of mature beech and oak forests grow in the shelter of the cliffs. The flat, wet areas below the bluffs, support horsetail ferns and mosses and even rarer plants such as adder's tongue fern.

Conducted nature walks are offered.

Ravine Creek Trail

Interpretive guide   Easy   45 minutes   1 km

This loop travels over a 2-m-wide earth path and boardwalk with two sets of stairs. The trail is routed through a ravine and a woodlot, and there are 11 stops explaining the geology, and local flora and fauna.

Beach Trail

Hiking   Easy   1 hour   2 km (return)

This linear, 2-m-wide trail travels over an earth surface to the sandy beach area of the park. The trail descends and ascends a 50-m bluff. A lookout point provides you with a spectacular view of Lake Erie, the beach area and the ravine.

ROCK POINT PROVINCIAL PARK

Box 158, Dunnville, Ontario N1A 2X5

Information: Call 905 774-6642
             Fax 905 774-3267

Operating season: May to October

Location: The park is on Lake Erie, 11 km south of Dunnville. Follow Regional Road 3 south to Niece Road. Travel west and the park is on your left.

Natural features: Wooded areas, rocky coasts, old fields and good beaches are some of the natural features found in this tract of former farmland on the shores of Lake Erie. Plants rarely found in the rest of Ontario, like shagbark hickories and blue beeches grow in the park.

Fossils embedded in the limestone shelves along the shore indicate that corals and reef organisms lived here in abundance 385 million years ago. There have been 267 bird species recorded in the park, and it's becoming a very popular place for birdwatchers. In the fall, huge numbers of monarch butterflies rest in the park before making their way across the lake.

Conducted nature walks are offered.

Woodlot Trail

Hiking   Easy   2 hours   5 km (return)

This linear trail with a small loop at its end, is 1.0 m wide with a surface primarily of sand and earth-clay. Walking becomes difficult in certain areas after rain. The trail travels through a variety of different environments within the park, along the top of a lakeside bluff, through old fields and into a Carolinian woodlot. Stairs can be taken down the side of the bluff to access the beach or limestone shelf with its many fossils. Or you can visit the viewing platform that overlooks Lake Erie and nearby Mohawk Island and lighthouse.

RONDEAU PROVINCIAL PARK
R.R. 1, Morpeth, Ontario N0P 1X0

Operating season: Open all year

Information: Call 519 674-1750
                       519 674-5405
                Fax 519 674-1755

Location: The park is located near the western basin of Lake Erie, southeast of Chatham. Access is via Highways 3 and 401, taking Exit 101 at Kent County Road 15.

Natural features: The park is famous for its lush Carolinian Forest with over 800 species of vegetation and unusual assortment of wildlife. Sassafras and tulip trees, tall bellflower — all species usually found much further south — are common in the park. The showy orchid is one of 19 reported species growing here. Approximately 134 of the 334 bird species recorded in the park nest here. Nesting birds include bald eagles, northern mockingbird and, among the endangered species, the prothonotary warbler. There are 33 types of mammals in the park such as the Virginia opossum and southern flying squirrel.

The park lies in long parallel ridges interspersed with valley-like depressions called sloughs. The park's dunes and pine and oak forests are dynamic ecosystems, where such interesting species as the five-linked skink, eastern hognosed snake and red-headed woodpecker can be observed. The sloughs and marshes around the bay are home to 30 types of reptiles and amphibians such as eastern spiny softshell turtle, spring peeper and bullfrog.

Three trails are linear, 2.5-m-wide abandoned roadways, while the other three are looped, with a width of 1.5 m. They run over earth path and/or boardwalk surfaces. Organized school tours and conducted nature walks are offered. Three of the trails allow cycling.

Tulip Tree Trail*

Hiking	Barrier-free	1 hour	1 km

Travelling over compacted limestone fines and on boardwalks bridging sloughs, this trail gives you a close-up view of how the park was formed. Hikers journey through pine and oak, and beech and maple forests. There are also examples of unique, Carolinian trees: tulip trees, sassafras, pumpkin ash and shagbark hickory. The tulip tree, the largest hardwood in North America, is easily located and touched along the trail.

Another significant aspect of the trail is the chance to see the endangered prothonotary warbler. Recent surveys indicate there are fewer than 20 nesting pairs in Ontario. The park is home to approximately half of these birds. Plans are afoot to have a trail guide available in the near future.

* Al's Picks, see page 164.

Spicebush Trail

Hiking	Barrier-free	1 hour	1.5 km

Winding through a southern hardwood forest, this trail is one of the best bird-watching locations in the park. The scents, sights and sounds along this trail will provide many lasting memories of the park. The travelling surface is of compacted limestone fines and boardwalk.

Black Oak Trail

Hiking   Easy   1 hour   1.4 km

The route traverses a narrow strip of pine and oak, and two meadow-like openings in the dense forest, while following an earth path. There are several types of oak trees growing near the trail.

Marsh Trail

Hiking   Easy   6 hours   14.4 km (return)

This linear trail travels on a gravel roadway through the heart of a marsh where wildlife abounds. The trail starts with forest and halfway down the roadway it opens up for a view of the vast marshland, which comprises approximately one third of the park's area. The marsh is dominated by wild rice, cattails and water lilies. Common birds sighted along this trail are eastern kingbirds, yellow warblers, black tern and marsh wrens. During the spring and fall thousands of waterfowl can be observed feeding on the wild rice. The trail is exceptional for watching frogs and turtles.

South Point Trail

Hiking   Easy   2 hours   8 km

This looped trail follows an unpaved roadway through a variety of forest habitats until reaching the point where it winds along the shoreline of Lake Erie for a short distance. This is a great place to see red-headed woodpeckers, southern flying squirrels and woodcock.

Harrison Trail

Hiking   Easy   3 hours   16 km (return)

Through the centre of the park a linear gravel roadway passes by a variety of habitats. Watch for wildlife such as birds, deer and raccoons, in the meadows and savannahs.

SAUBLE FALLS PROVINCIAL PARK

R.R. 3, Wiarton, Ontario N0H 2T0

Operating season: April to October

Information: Call 519 422-1952
Fax 519 422-1149

Location: The park is on the Lake Huron side of the Bruce Peninsula, along Bruce County Road 13, midway between Sauble Beach and Oliphant.

Natural features: The centrepiece of the park, Sauble Falls, descends in tiers over rough and jagged dolomite, a type of limestone typical of the Niagara Escarpment. Much of the original red and white pine and other species was harvested in the last century. Huge stumps can be seen amidst the second-growth mixed forest. An array of delicate orchids and ferns grow here. Throughout June and July, bright orange wood lilies can be found in the dry, sandy environment of the dunes. Birdwatchers may see many songbirds and shorebirds, especially during spring and fall migrations.

There are two trails, both 2.5 m wide. In winter, park roads may be used for cross-country skiing and snowshoeing.

Sauble Trail

Interpretive guide   Easy   1 hour   2.5 km

This looped trail travels over earth and sand surfaces through a plantation of predominantly red pine. Parts of the trail are next to the Sauble River. There are a few steep grades to climb, and there are eight interpretive stops explaining present and past forest management practices in this area.

Falls Viewing Trail and Boardwalk Trail

Interpretive displays   Easy   30 minutes   0.5 km

This linear trail is located on both sides of the Sauble River. The north side has a compacted limestone fines surface, leading to a viewing platform overlooking the falls. The access is generally barrier-free, but some assistance may be needed. The south side is accessed by stairs to a boardwalk running parallel to the river. At the entrance to this area there are interpretive display panels explaining the historical importance of the site.

SELKIRK PROVINCIAL PARK
R.R. 1, Selkirk, Ontario N0A 1P0

Information: Call 905 776-2600
Fax 519 426-5268

Operating Season: May to October

Location: On the north shore of Lake Erie, about 20 km east of Port Dover.

Natural features: The land is former farmland. Blue grass, devil's paintbrush, chicory, and St. John's wort are some of the plants and wildflowers that grow beneath the red and white oaks, maples, cherry trees, ash and shagbark hickories. White-tailed deer, raccoons, rabbits, squirrels and 224 species of marsh and shore bird have been observed in the park.

Wheeler's Walk Trail

Hiking   Easy   1 hour   2 km

This looped trail is 1.0 m wide with a walking surface of earth, gravel and boardwalk. The trail winds through a forest of oaks, maples and shagbark hickory and pine. A short boardwalk spans the marsh, providing a close-up look at the wetland environment, which includes plants such as arrowhead, water lilies and cattails.

SPRINGWATER PROVINCIAL PARK
Midhurst, Ontario L0L 1X0

Information: Call 705 728-7393
Fax 705 728-5444

Operating season: Open all year

Location: The park is 10 km northwest of Barrie, on Highway 26.

Natural features: The park is mainly forested with some open areas, streams and ponds. A variety of native wildlife, animals that were once injured or orphaned, can be seen in the park. The pine forests shelter many delicate wildflowers and plants such as jack-in-the-pulpit or lady's slipper. The hermit thrush and yellow-billed cuckoo, although unusual in the area, nest here, along with hairy woodpeckers, pine warblers and others.

Visitors learn about wildlife by using the displays set up along the trails. There are three cross-country ski trails used as short hiking trails. There are no hiking trail maps or guides, but a cross-country ski trail map is available. Five of the trails are looped. All the trails are between 1.0 m and 2 m in width, travelling mostly over an earth path. Other trail uses permitted are mountain-biking, cross-country skiing and snowshoeing.

William R. Wilson Trail

Interpretive guide   Easy   45 minutes   1.5 km

This trail travels over earth path and boardwalk, through natural and plantation forest. It is specially designed for children. There are 14 interpretive stops focussing on woodland animals.

Animal Display Trail

Interpretive displays Barrier-free   1 hour   1 km

Specially constructed for wheelchairs, baby strollers or those who have difficulty walking, this paved trail accesses 16 interpretive display panels discussing human and wildlife interaction. Animals native to Ontario are showcased.

Using cross-country ski trails and a map, the following three short hiking trails are provided.

Wildlife Trail

Hiking   Moderate   1.5 hours   2.5 km

The trail travels over earth path and unpaved road surfaces through pine plantations and naturally forested areas.

Woodland Trail

Hiking   Moderate   2 hours   4 km

Travelling over earth path, meadow, field, and unpaved road, and through forests of pine, maple and oak, this trail has a number of significant grades to climb and descend. It connects to the long-distance Ganaraska Hiking Trail.

Nursery Trail

Hiking   Strenuous   3 hours   6 km (return)

This linear trail travels over earth path and unpaved road surfaces. You will walk through two types of forest — a cedar and ash forest and a mature red and white pine plantation — with some significant grades to climb and descend.

TURKEY POINT PROVINCIAL PARK

Box 5, Turkey Point, Ontario N0E 1T0

Information: Call 519 426-3239
                      Fax 519 426-5268

Operating season: May to October

Location: The park is on Lake Erie, east of Long Point. Take Regional Road 10 southeast from Highway 24 and follow the signs.

Natural features: The park contains vegetation typical of the Carolinian forest region, as well as extensive areas of plantations. Tree species such as tulip, sassafras, chestnut and flowering dogwood grow abundantly. A 21-hectare nature reserve has been set aside to protect a significant plant community.

The high bluff in the park supports a pine and oak forest, including a savannah of old black oak. Halfway down the bluff, a wide variety of plants are found, many of them now rare and endangered. Birds such as whip-poor-wills and hermit thrush are found here. The wild turkey, from which the park derives its name, has been reintroduced in the past 15 years and many of them roam the forests in and around the park.

There are three trails. Two of them are loops and 1.5 m wide. Conducted nature walks are offered. Other trail uses are mountain biking and cross-country skiing.

Rainbow Ridge Trail

Interpretive guide   Easy   1 hour   2.4 km

Travelling over an earth path, boardwalk and sand surface, the trail passes by Potter's Creek and the Hatchery Pond. Along the trail ten interpretive stops explain the ecology of the park's marsh and woodland. You will see lots of chipmunks.

Fin and Feather Trail

Hiking	Moderate	1 hour	3 km (return)

This linear trail is 1.5 m wide, and travels over earth, unpaved road and sand through a red pine plantation, arriving at the Normandale Fish Culture Station. There are three short, steep grades to climb.

Bluff Lookout Trail

Interpretive guide	Easy	1 hour	2.2 km

There are ten interpretive stops explaining how humans use the natural landscape. The trail leads to a bluff overlooking the village of Turkey Point and Long Point Bay.

WASAGA BEACH PROVINCIAL PARK
Box 183, Wasaga Beach, Ontario L0L 2P0

Information: Call 705 429-2516
Fax 705 429-7983

Operating season: Open all year

Location: The park lies around the town of Wasaga Beach, on the south shore of Georgian Bay, along Nottawasaga Bay. It is accessible via Highways 26 or 92.

Natural features: Wasaga Beach is well-known for its white sand beaches, the longest freshwater beaches in the world. The ancient beach ridges called transverse dunes were formed by the prevailing northwest winds. Wind and weather gradually shifted sand from these ridges forming parabolic or U-shaped dunes. These high, steep-sloped mounds of sand are the largest known set of undisturbed parabolic dunes in Ontario, and their well-developed, well-preserved and accessible location makes them unique in the Great Lakes region. Vegetation such as yellow puccoon, New Jersey tea, and a rare arctic flower, Hobell's rock cress help stabilize the dunes. Sightings of deer, porcupine and raccoon are common. There have been 232 species of bird identified in the park, among them plovers, sandpipers and sanderlings.

There is one short hiking trail located away from the beach area but still within the park. The trail is crossed by the long distance Ganaraska Hiking Trail. There are six cross-country ski trails in this area and a bicycling trail near the beach. Conducted nature walks and school tours are available.

Blueberry Plains Trail

Hiking	Easy	1 hour	4 km

This looped hiking trail is a cross-country ski trail during the winter. It is cleared to approximately 2 m wide. The trail traverses sand dunes, and passes through vegetation such as red maple and white cedar on the tops of these ridges and white birch and red ash at the bottom. The trail leaves the forest and passes over the unique parabolic dunes before re-entering the wooded area and returning to the beginning.

Boardwalk Trail

Hiking	Barrier-free	45 minutes	0.8 km

This linear, 3-m-wide boardwalk runs parallel to the beachfront of Georgian Bay providing access to beach areas 1 and 2.

Ganaraska Hiking Trail

Hiking	Easy	3 hours	14.8km

This linear, 1–2-m earth and sand trail can be accessed from a number of different locations. The route crosses the post-Nipissing raised beaches and transverse dunes. The Wasaga-Ganaraska Hiking Club conducts weekly group hikes on sections of the trail.

OTHER SPECIAL PLACES

Mono Cliffs Provincial Park
There are seven interpretive trails (a total 21.5 km), offering opportunities to look at province-specific plants with the added bonus of spectacular views especially during fall colours. For more information, write or call Earl Rowe Provincial Park.

Boyne Valley Provincial Park
There are three interpretive trails (a total of 11 km) to provide visitors with picturesque views of the Boyne River Valley. For more information, call or write to Earl Rowe Provincial Park.

Hockley Valley Provincial Nature Reserve
There are three hiking trails (a total of 14 km) at their best during the fall colours. For more information, call or write to Earl Rowe Provincial Park.

Short Hills Provincial Park
There are ten trails (a total of 23 km), both interpretive and hiking. Most of the trails are easy to walk, with viewing platforms, boardwalks and bridges along the way. The park offers such natural features as mature deciduous trees, waterfalls and unique plants. For more information, write to the Friends of Short Hills Provincial Park (address at the back of this book).

Forks of the Credit Provincial Park
There are four trails (a total of 8 km). All are interpretive, half are easy to walk, and the other half moderately easy. You will see the Cataract Falls, ruins of a mill, early settlers' farmstead, and be able to explore the bottomlands of the Credit River Valley. For more information, call or write to Earl Rowe Provincial Park.

Trillium Woods Provincial Park
The park has a profuse and dramatic show of unusual types of trilliums each spring. Growing within a mature hardwood forest dominated by black cherry trees, the blossoms are spectacular. For more information, call or write to Port Burwell Provincial Park.

AL'S PICKS

Bronte Creek Provincial Park: Half Moon Valley Trail

Surrounded by millions of people, this island of green lets visitors experience the natural and historic aspects of Bronte Creek. The creek itself is a wide stream flowing through a deep valley, thick with second-growth forest, towards Lake Ontario. It has substantial seasonal populations of silver coho and Chinook salmon, rainbow and brook trout, and some smallmouth bass. The Half Moon Valley Trail is the only trail that leads to the creek and to where some aboriginal people lived until 1820.

The trail has two interconnecting loops. A main loop travels down three terraces, created over centuries by receding water levels, to a lookout platform overlooking the creek and valley. From here the trail returns past a deep and completely buried ravine. This is an unusual landform which we rarely have the opportunity of seeing. The trail guide provides a clear description as to how this phenomenon happened. Equally interesting is a hidden cave carved out of the rock. It is believed that this cave was the hiding place for William Lyon McKenzie during the fight for Toronto, then York, in 1837. The cave is not visible from the trail.

The trail continues through a forested area of evergreens, and before long the canopy opens and you are walking across an open field. This has signs of a new forest growing out of an agricultural past. Near its exit the trail joins up with a cycling and walking path. Keep left and you will return to the start of the trail.

Half Moon Valley Trail at Bronte Creek.

The second, or valley loop is accessed from the main loop, on the right about ten minutes from the start of the trail. Listen carefully for the sound of running water. Using a wooden stairway, this route descends 38 m to the valley floor close to the creek. On the right at the bottom of the stairs, a small brick kiln operated here between 1849 and 1874, providing bricks for many of the buildings found in the park.

Now reduce your pace so you can appreciate the details of this half-moon-shaped valley carved and deepened by water. You are now in the middle of Half Moon Valley. The hillside above the trail to your right rises quickly and steeply, and a short distance ahead you will come to a small marsh. It is worth stopping on the boardwalk and taking the time to look carefully at the plants and wildlife unfolding in this green maze. Watch for signs of raccoons, white-tailed deer or birds such as the blue jay. Trees and plants not normally found in southern Ontario, such as red ash, tamarack and sphagnum moss grow well in this moist and sheltered environment.

The trail turns away from the marsh to hug the creek shoreline. (It's interesting to note that the creek was once dammed in order to operate a major sawmill.) It then leaves the creek and returns to the main trail. At this point you have a choice of returning to the start of the trail by turning left, or continuing your walk along the main trail, by turning right.

Pinery Provincial Park: Heritage Trail

Only 100 years ago, Pinery was a small segment of the natural landscape of Ontario. Today it is the largest remaining single piece of forested land in southwestern Ontario. The 3-km Heritage Trail provides a historical review of the struggle to protect and conserve such a special place.

This well-signed, well-constructed and barrier-free trail is a pleasure to walk. What makes it even more pleasurable is the interpretive trail guide available at the trailhead. Inexpensive, full colour and pocket sized, the guide is full of interesting facts about the park and the people who made Pinery Provincial Park what it is today.

The trail is located in the northeast section of the park. It meanders through an area best known for some of the most extensive rare oak savannah habitat left in North America. As you walk along this wide, flat trail you will see the typical open canopy, and well spaced, black and red oak trees of the savannah, but very little undergrowth. The lack of undergrowth is a major problem for the survival of this rare habitat. There have been no fires since the 1950s and the large deer population has prevented very little regeneration. However, remedial steps were taken in 1990 using a controlled burn in the area, and in 1998 the park's deer herd was reduced by 264 animals. These measures should result in an increase in natural regeneration and, it's hoped, survival of this rare habitat.

This all-season trail offers a variety of natural enjoyment. In the spring, the trail leads you through an area glowing with prairie ragwort, an attractive yellow wildflower typical of the oak savannah. During the summer you can see white-tailed deer, flying squirrels and owls. In the winter, the snow on the trail is packed, allowing for hiking and sightings of abundant wildlife tracks.

By using the trail guide, the 12 interpretive stops tell you the story of its human history. Just past stop 5 the trail turns right, a 0.6-km extension from the main trail leads you to a viewing platform and canoe dock overlooking the Old Ausable Channel. The lack of flow in the Old Ausable Channel today is the result of the building of a "cut" south of Pinery Park to divert water and drain the adjacent Thedford Bog. Cut off from its original source, the flow now in the Old Ausable Channel is a result of springs that continue to fill this old riverbed with clear water.

Returning from the channel keep right, and from this point you are about 20 minutes away from the start of the trail. As you walk along watch for the variety of birdlife or look to the side of trail in the sandy soil for wildlife tracks from white-tailed deer and raccoons. But remember to stay on the trails, as poison ivy is common in the park.

After absorbing the fascinating natural and cultural history of the area, take a moment to reflect on what we can learn from our mistakes, and more importantly, what we can do to protect our natural heritage in the future.

Rondeau Provincial Park: Tulip Tree Trail

This is a short, easy, barrier-free trail with viewing platforms, providing excellent close-up access to some of Canada's unique flora and fauna such as the Carolinian tulip and sassafras trees. The wet forest terrain is threaded with extensive sections of wide boardwalk and in drier sections the dense shrubbery makes this an excellent birding trail. Bring along your binoculars, camera and insect repellent.

Starting out from the parking lot near the visitor centre, the trail winds gently through a small area of pine, to arrive at the first boardwalk section, crossing a slough (pronounced "slew"). These sloughs, as well as the higher drier ridges allow for the growth of a wide diversity of plant and wildlife, ranging from pine and oak forests to beech and maple forests with spicebush and dogwood shrubbery. The slough also provides an environment for insects such as mosquitoes and dragonflies, that spend the early stages of their lives in water.

On reaching the second boardwalk, one of the trees that the trail is named after — the tulip tree — can be easily seen and touched. It is the largest hardwood tree in North America. In Ontario, it grows to a height of 36 m. Mature trees may lack branches for the first 18 m and this, together with its massive, straight trunk and shiny green leaves, makes the tulip tree impressive indeed.

Just past this boardwalk you reach a trail junction where you can chose either to return to the visitor centre by using a shorter version of the trail, or to continue. By continuing along the trail you will see many more tall tulip trees, amongst the elephant trees or blue beech, pumpkin trees, (pumpkin ash) and sugar maple. The root systems of many plants are shallow in the sandy soil. This provides very little anchorage against strong winds, ice and snow storms. During the summer of 1998 many trees were toppled during a severe gale that closed the park for seven days. Take your time, and you will notice old and new snags of beech trees slowly disintegrating among some fine straight tulip trees.

The trail continues to wind over drier ridges until reaching two long sections of boardwalk. Along here if you are walking quietly in the spring or early summer don't be alarmed by the sound of a duck taking off from the water venting its surprise by crying out in an ascending whistle. It is probably the wood duck. The male wood duck is one of Canada's most handsome ducks and is the only duck at Rondeau to build its nest in a tree. Meanwhile, a shrill five-note whistle may be heard from the shrubbery nearby and this would be the rare prothonotary warbler, a bird with a yellow head and breast, and grey-blue wings. Also, if you're here in spring, be sure to bring a wildflower guidebook for identifying the plants. Even the tulip tree has a flower of greenish-yellow with an orange ring at its base.

Slowly the trail works its way back through the mature woods, passing over more sloughs. All too soon the trail has completed its circuit and you are back where you started. Be sure to stop in at the Visitor Centre next to the trail. Besides getting answers to some of your trail questions, it is an excellent opportunity to learn more about the park's natural and cultural features.

The Tulip Trail at Rondeau Provincial Park.

Ontario Trail Associations and Friends

Ontario Trail Associations

Bruce Trail Association
Box 857
Hamilton, Ontario
L8N 3N9
www.brucetrail.org

Ganaraska Trail Association
12 King Street
Box 19
Orillia, Ontario
L3V 1R1
www3.sympatico.ca/hikers.net/ganarask

Hike Ontario
Suite 411
1185 Eglinton Ave East
North York, Ontario
M3C 3C6
www3.sympatico.ca/hikers.net/hikeont

Ontario Trails Council
Trails Studies Unit
Trent University
Peterborough, Ontario
K9J 7B8

Rideau Trail Association
Box 15
Kingston, Ontario
K7L 4V6
www.ncf.carleton.ca/RTA

Voyageur Trail Association
Box 20040
150 Churchill Blvd
Sault Ste. Marie, Ontario
P6A 6W3
www3.sympatico.ca/voyageur.trail

Waterfront Regeneration Trust
Waterfront Trail
207 Queen's Quay West
Box 129
Toronto, Ontario
M5J 1A7
www.waterfronttrail.org

Friends of Ontario Provincial Parks

Friends of Algonquin Park
Box 248
Whitney, Ontario
K0J 2M0
www.algonquinpark.on.ca/friends

Friends of Awenda Park
c/o Awenda Provincial Park
Box 973
Penetanguishene, Ontario
L0K 1P0

Friends of Bon Echo Park
Box 229
Cloyne, Ontario
K0H 1K0
www.mazinaw.on.ca/fobecho

Friends of Bonnechere Parks
Box 220
Pembroke, Ontario
K8A 6X4
www.limestone.edu.on.ca/
mackayr/frndsbon.htm

Friends of Bronte Creek Park
c/o Bronte Creek Provincial Park
1219 Burloak Drive
Burlington, Ontario
L7R 3X5

Friends of Charleston Lake Park
R.R. 4
Lansdowne, Ontario
K0E 1L0
www.fcbe.edu.on.ca/~mackayr/frndscha

Friends of French River Heritage Park
732 McIntyre Street West
North Bay, Ontario
P1B 2Z9

Friends of Frontenac Park
Box 129
Sydenham, Ontario
K0H 2T0
www.fcbe.edu.on.ca/Frontenacpark/Friends

Friends of Killarney Park
General Delivery
Killarney, Ontario
P0M 2A0

Niijkiwenhwag-Friends of Lake Superior Park
c/o Lake Superior Provincial Park
Box 267
Wawa, Ontario
P0S 1K0

Friends of MacGregor Point Park
c/o MacGregor Point Provincial Park
R.R. 1
Port Elgin, Ontario
N0H 2C5

Friends of Mattawa River Heritage Park
c/o Samuel de Champlain Provincial Park
Box 147
Mattawa, Ontario
P0H 1V0

Friends of Misery Bay
R.R. 1
Manitouwaning, Ontario
P0P 1N0

The Friends of Mississagi Park
Box 552
Elliot Lake, Ontario
P5A 2J9

Friends of Murphys Point Park
c/o Murphys Point Provincial Park
R.R. 5
Perth, Ontario
K7H 3C7

Friends of Ojibway Prairie Park
Ojibway Nature Centre
5200 Matchette Road
Windsor, Ontario
N9C 4E8

Friends of Pinery Park
R.R. 2
Grand Bend, Ontario
N0M 1T0

Friends of Quetico Park
Box 1959
Atikokan, Ontario
P0T 1C0

Friends of Presqu'ile Park
Box 1442
Brighton, Ontario
K0K 1H0

The Friends of Rondeau Park
R.R. 1
Morpeth, Ontario
N0P 1X0

Friends of Rushing River Park
Box 5160
Kenora, Ontario
P9N 3X9

Friends of Sandbanks Park
Box 20007
219 Main Street
Picton, Ontario
K0K 3V0

Friends of Short Hills Park
c/o The St. John's Outdoor Studies Centre
2984 Holland Road, R.R.1
Fonthill, Ontario
L0S 1E6
www.vaxxine.com/buzzworld/sub/friends.eht

Friends of Sleeping Giant Park
Box 29031
McIntyre Centre Postal Outlet
1186 Memorial Avenue
Thunder Bay, Ontario
P7B 6P9

Friends of Wasaga Park
Box 183
Wasaga Beach, Ontario
L0L 2P0

The Friends of White Otter Castle
Box 88
Atikokan, Ontario
P0T 1C0

Recommended Reading

Cundiff, Brad and Evert Hilkers. *The Hike Ontario Guide to Walks Around Toronto.* Boston Mills Press, 1994.

Elder, John, ed. *Nature/Ralph Waldo Emerson. Walking/Henry David Thoreau.* Beacon Press, Massachusetts, 1991.

Gregory, Dan and Roderick Mackenzie. *Toronto's Backyard: A Guide to Selected Nature Walks.* Douglas and McIntyre, 1986.

Griffin, Steven A. and Elizabeth May. *Hiking for Kids: A Family Hiking Guide.* Northword Press, Wisconsin, 1996.

Hickman, Pamela. *In the Woods: Exploring, Discovering, Observing, Playing, Crafts.* Formac Publishing, 1998.

Hike Ontario. *Walking and Hiking in Ontario: Hike Ontario Fact Sheets.* North York, 1995.

Katz, Elliott. *The Complete Guide to Walking In Canada.* Doubleday, 1991.

Ontario Parks. *Parks Guide.* Queens Printer, Toronto,1998.

Patton, Brian and Bart Robinson. *The Canadian Rockies Trail Guide. Fifth Edition* Summerthought, 1992.

Robertson, Doug. *The Best Hiking in Ontario.* Hurtig Publishers, 1992.

Runtz, Michael. *The Explorer's Guide To Algonquin Park.* Stoddart Publishing, 1993.

Teasdale, Shirley. *Hiking Ontario's Heartland.* Whitecap Books, 1993.

Wake, Winifred. *A Nature Guide to Ontario.* Federation of Ontario Naturalists, University of Toronto Press, 1997.

Waterfront Regeneration Trust. *The Waterfront Trail — Explore Yesterday, Today and Tomorrow along the Shores of Lake Ontario.* Webcom Ltd., 1995.